THE BASEBALL MIRACLE OF THE *Splendid 6* AND TOWNY TOWNSEND

PATRICK MONTGOMERY

FOREWORD BY DAVID WRIGHT

SEVEN-TIME MLB ALL-STAR AND A MEMBER OF THE SPLENDID 6

The Baseball Miracle of the Splendid 6 and Towny Townsend

ISBN: 978-1-66784-854-9
eBook ISBN: 978-1-66784-855-6

Every baseball player is a combination of who they were coached by, who they played with and who they watched on TV.

—Baseballism

CONTENTS

Foreword....1

Author's Introduction....4

One: The Tidewater Baseball Miracle....14

Two: Baseball Forgotten And Reborn....16

Three: Baseball Beginnings....22

Four: The Man, The Myth, The Towny....25

Five: The Baseball Wife....31

Six: Towny And His Extraordinary Teammates....40

Seven: A Baseball Crown Prince....44

Eight: Giving Back....50

Nine: Blasters And Drillers....53

Ten: Never Tell Me The Odds....68

Eleven: Youth Baseball, Or Youth Playing Baseball?....73

Twelve: Dismal Swamp....78

Thirteen: One Time At Baseball Camp....82

Fourteen: Through Parents' Eyes 95

Fifteen: Tidewater Loyalty 105

Sixteen: A Path Not Taken 111

Seventeen: The Showcase 119

Eighteen: David Wright 130

Nineteen: Ryan Zimmerman 136

Twenty: B.J. Upton 143

Twenty-One: Justin Upton 151

Twenty-Two: Mark Reynolds 155

Twenty-Three: Michael Cuddyer 163

Twenty-Four: Passing The Torch 171

Twenty-Five: Cooperstown 182

Twenty-Six: Babe Ruth—Baseball Hero And Cancer Pioneer 200

Twenty-Seven: Towny And A Long Goodbye 204

FOREWORD

By David Wright,
Seven-Time MLB All-Star and a Member of the Splendid 6

The stories of baseball heroes are told and retold. But the Major League Baseball players do not come from Central Casting or a laboratory. Players love the game, and we get the love from someone like you. Players spend thousands of hours in drills, practice, and games. Parents and coaches drive players countless miles to games everywhere and throw, hit, and field with the child until the last of the lights go out. Each player needs to love the game and have the skills and mental makeup to play it at their highest level. It is a journey nobody can do alone. I know I didn't.

This book by Patrick Montgomery is not just about baseball players; it is really about the legacy of why boys and girls pick up a glove, throw a ball for the first time, and the passing of the game from one generation to another. Parents, family, friends, coaches, or whomever you are blessed to cross paths with, placed that glove into your hand for the first time.

There are so many gracious and selfless people in my life whom very few people have ever heard of outside the Hampton Roads area of Virginia. People I admire and who helped instill the passion and determination for me to become a Major League Baseball player and a better and a complete person.

My parents, Rhon and Elisa, always did everything they could, often sacrificing, so my brothers, Stephen, Matthew, Daniel, and I could track down whatever ball was bouncing that particular time of year. As a result, I had the gift and latitude of focusing on my grades and my sports as a teenager. I certainly know how lucky I am to have parents like Rhon and Elisa Wright, and my brothers' support blended in with a few hard sit-downs to correct my course if my head swelled too large.

Coach Townsend introduced me to the "game within the game" of baseball. He taught me and so many other Hampton Roads' kids life lessons through baseball and ensured I was in the basepath of success. Coach Erbe is another one of those coaches I will always be thankful to have in my life. His attention to detail is second to none, and his baseball IQ is off the charts. There is no doubt that his love for the game and tireless work ethic rubbed off on me and my teammates.

Baseball is a living legacy capable of bridging across generations. All it needs is picking up a glove for the first time and playing a simple game of catch. The players you see on television or at the stadium are in love with the game as much as you and started by just picking up a glove. The people in this book are why I love the game the way I do. Never be too old or too busy for a good game of catch!

As Towny Townsend said over and over during his life: *Baseball people are the best kind of people.*

—David Wright

AUTHOR'S INTRODUCTION

Towny Townsend is a name few know outside a small region of Virginia. However, millions unwittingly observed his fingerprints all-over Major-League Baseball. Baseball during the last several decades displayed Towny's grace and impact each time players like David Wright, Michael Cuddyer, Mark Reynolds, Ryan Zimmerman, B.J., and Justin Upton were able to keep their bat in the hitting zone for an impossibly long extra microsecond turning a strike into a base hit, or a seemingly impossible play pulled out of the dirt to save the team. It is no accident or coincidence a crop of baseball greatness bloomed from the same fertile lands that once was the cradle of the New World. Seemingly ordinary kids turned into baseball players ready for the highest levels of baseball and life. Towny Townsend served as a baseball Godfather, visionary, and facilitator along with his friends, coaches, and the parents of the players making baseball greatness and along the way, changing the shape and destiny of several Major League teams for decades.

I was not a friend or "teammate" of Towny Townsend. Though I would have been honored to be so if ever having the chance. I first heard of Towny Townsend and some of the extraordinary ballplayers being developed in Tidewater when I reported to the Coast Guard's Mid-Atlantic Command (LANTAREA) in Portsmouth, Virginia. The Command is responsible for overseeing Coast Guard Districts up and down the East Coast, the Midlands, and parts of Europe.

As an Active-Duty Coast Guard Public Affairs Specialist First Class reporting in the week after 9/11, I reported in during a hectic and scary time for everyone. Baseball represents normalcy to me, and I always looked to it as a stabilizing force, and I needed that Mike Piazza blast into the night the first game after 9/11, and I beamed with pride as President Bush threw out the first pitch before game 3 of the World Series that stretched into November.

Baseball was always something I loved to follow, especially the players from the area I lived in. I knew of basketball players like Alonzo Mourning, Allen Iverson, and Ron Curry from Hampton Roads. I also learned to love Roger Brown's Restaurant and Sports Bar (emphasis on the Sports Bar for me) just a couple of blocks away from the Coast Guard Building in Portsmouth. Roger Brown was a great retired NFL player from the somewhat close town of Surry. I love the other sports and appreciated them, but I wanted to learn about baseball in the area. Names like Michael Cuddyer, who was just trying to cut his teeth with the Twins, and David Wright, who was just selected by the Mets, kept coming up. And a local phenomenon named B.J. Upton, and a player who would possibly surpass all of them—the younger Justin Upton—were local baseball conversations at the time. The Tidewater area was buzzing with the names of kids on the verge of making it in baseball, and I liked it.

Baseball geekdom is hard to lose, even as you are pushing past 30, with a wife and a tiny infant girl. My daughter Samantha took in her first baseball game in the mid-summer with the oppressive heat and humidity of New Orleans. Bringing my three-week-old daughter to sit a few rows off the field in our season holder tickets for the New Orleans Zephyrs the summer of 2001 did not win my wife, Barbara, and I the Parents of the Year award. However, we were and still are baseball people. So in 2002, living in Portsmouth, as we were getting ready to transfer to Atlantic City, New Jersey, we made a point to be sitting in the first row of the third base side to have the best view, with our daughter, of the Tidewater Tides.

Several years later, my man-crush on Derek Jeter had us take our growing family, now with two daughters, Samantha and Billy to see the Yankees at Camden Yards and sit in the best seats our meager salaries couldn't really afford, to introduce our kids to the Yankees, the subtle greatness of Derek Jeter, and more importantly Major League Baseball. It was an investment that paid off well as our daughters ended up playing softball up until college, and can easily debate baseball and the players to anyone.

Baseball fans just love baseball. It is that kind of love that coaches like Towny Townsend, Allan Erbe, Matt Sinnen, and Gary Wright helped to instill into their players more efficiently and perhaps safer, than I did taking infants or toddlers to baseball games. But the love for baseball led me to the memory of Towny Townsend.

Cathy Townsend is a woman of strength, simple truths, and a fierce, loyal love for Towny Townsend. I knew if I were to write about the Splendid 6 of Tidewater, the story would have to begin with Towny Townsend. Without Towny, there probably would not have been the framework and lanes for the great players to learn and grow. Lee Banks, with his Amazing Mets Showcase team with the arguably most talented amateur team ever compiled, would not have happened.

In between takes of a Rap Music Video shoot for the up-and-coming musician, A. Starr, I tried reaching Cathy Townsend after thumbing through my phone, grasping at any straws and threads that may lead to contacting her. My role as the gym coach for the video allowed me time to shoot off a text, an email, and voice-mail into what I thought may be an abyss and maybe a restraining order. My stomach ached, and anxiety swept over me on the whole way home of the eight-hour drive from Nashville to Columbia, South Carolina.

I knew the story of Coach Townsend, and these players needed to be told. The Splendid 6 were well known already, but I had the absolute need gnawing deep to show the…and? What else? It wouldn't happen if my phone did not chirp, and soon.

Days turned into almost a week. As I was looking at other approaches to Cathy Townsend and feeling more than a little discouraged on how to tell the story without Towny, the phone finally chirped. I received a call from 757 area code. It was Cathy Townsend, the widow of Towny Townsend. The voice on the phone was hesitant, curious, and almost surprised. She was willing to talk about her husband for a book. Cathy Townsend, like her husband, would not be one to take lightly or trifle with. After all the years, the feeling of love and respect she still felt for Towny was palpable and humbling.

I have something in common with Justin Upton. I too was once the first pick in a baseball draft. I was the 1984 No. 1 Selection of the Junior Minor Baseball League in Key West, Florida. Like the Splendid 6, I was a shortstop, and that was perhaps the highest note hit during my amateur athletic career. My high school wrestling career was record-breaking, though. I probably hold the New Jersey State record for the quickest pin. I don't think if David Wright hit me with a baseball bat, I could end up on my back and counted out faster. I picked myself up, bettered myself, and wrestled through my Senior year, even winning a match every now and then.

I moved to Key West as a 12-year-old from New York. I never was allowed to play on a youth team growing up because it didn't fit in with the Witness Protection Program my family may or may not have been in; or it was perhaps the attempts to evade the eyes of the Government. I was never sure; I was just happy years later to a hold Security Clearance. By the time I was 12, I had already lived in 14 different locations, and team sports were never an option. The new kid in town and at school, I always looked to the stability of baseball. Yes, my glove and baseball card collection always found its way into a repurposed moving box.

Being new and often dropped into a new school on some random afternoon never stopped me from finding games, whether in urban, suburban, or the rural areas I lived in. I would play as long as the sun or lightposts would allow. But Key West was going to be different. I knew I would have at least a few years in the tiny island town. I went to my first baseball tryout with high hopes.

I knew the shortstop was usually the best player, and my New York confidence was high that night as I took my spot for the tryout. Baseball Gods blessed me as I handled all the opportunities offered and even flashed a good arm that I knew I didn't have with my throws to first base. I was the Key West version of Bucky Dent. Now it was time to bat. I was built like a young David Wright, the

12-year-old version. I looked like the same pudgy Blaster, and I even showed some bat stroke for the tryout.

I went home that night happy and full of confidence that I would own the league as a player. The next day I got the call that TCI took me with the first pick. The coach was totally psyched to have me! The coach was a former Major League catcher with five days or so of Service Time but never made it into an actual game. He was Crash Davis before I ever saw Bull Durham.

I took my birthright—shortstop—and proceeded to boot every ball and bounce each throw to a slow roll to the first baseman during our first practice. The coach, a huge man with a wheelbarrow chest stuffed tightly into his 6-foot-2 frame, came out to me at shortstop and quietly asked me my name because I could not be the player he saw and selected as number one. But I was, and I began my walk of shame to start my youth sports career as a right fielder.

The highlight of my three years on the team was when I ducked out from a curveball strike, like the chubby kid I was, ditching for an ice cream truck. The whole team laughed their butts off. I stood back in, and the jerk ball pitcher tossed me the same pitch, hoping for an embarrassing replay, but this time it hung and I stayed in. I hit a frozen rope down the third base line and dove into third base headfirst with the best Pete Rose "belly flop" ever seen in the Florida Keys. It was real and it was fabulous.

The memories of my children being born, my wedding, and eating 13 meatballs each the size of a baseball at Castaldi's Italian restaurant in Norfolk with the waitstaff, kitchen workers, and some good friends cheering on my greatest athletic moment are all milestone-memories, but that triple is up in there somewhere.

Even the best coaches cannot make a kid a great player if the talent is not there. But the way my youth coaches treated me fed my competitive spirit, helped me make friends in a new town, and in general, taught me we are not always what we think we are, and that version is good to be, too. I am proud of each dribbler for a hit, every time leaning into a pitch or closing my four-foot-something frame to draw a walk to help the team. Little lessons mean the world to me now.

I am fine; my athletic career peaked unspectacularly and early in life. I am in the vast majority of those it happened to.

The thought of meeting Elisa and Rhon Wright, the parents of Stephen, Matthew, Daniel, and David Wright, terrified me. I have stood shoulder to shoulder with Admirals and Generals to brief on topics and have discussions they did not want to hear. But it was my duty, and I was okay with that; however, walking into the Wright family home was my choice and the first in-person interview for this book. As I sat in my truck a respectful non-stalker distance 15 minutes early near their house, feelings of excitement and "what the heck am I doing?" were percolating around my gut.

I did my required reading on Rhon and Elisa, and the thought of walking into a retired Assistant Chief of the Norfolk Police Department's house was eating me up. I was expecting a crusty old military type, bowing me up as I knocked on the door, perhaps judging me for making my best impression of Mr. Potato Head with my frumpy retired Coast Guard body. Instead, Rhon Wright opened the door with a big smile, glasses, and less hair than I had, and although clearly in shape, he did not have the body of a young Greek God. Maybe I was going to be okay.

My fears went on high alert as we sat down, and Elisa offered me coffee. After the first polite refusal, I knew it was best to take their hospitality. But the question of "how do you take your coffee" was about to rattle me. I stopped short of asking for two Splenda stirred counter-clockwise with lactose-free whole milk, preferably with a nice froth. I instead went with a safer "milk and sugar," the "regular" where I was raised around New York City. Rhon Wright's eyes opened wide, and he almost bellowed to me, "What military guy doesn't take coffee black?"

Rhon, of course, was right, and I knew it. Trying to change his eye level and gaze, made me want to spill the coffee and run out of the room; instead, I shifted uncomfortably in the chair and directed my eyes to a High School Senior portrait on the wall. "Wow, I can certainly see that is David." Boom, 0-2. Rhon and Elisa first gave me a stern look. The interview, in my mind, was on the rocks and the book with it. But as things often are, they are not what they appear. A smile emerged slowly, followed by laughter, telling me it was Matthew and giving me the correct names to the pictures and the reminder of a quiz later.

In my defense, my daughters are three years apart, and sometimes they look like twins to me and I mix up their pictures. However, Rhon and Elisa are among the sweetest, most friendly, and humble people I know. I think they were having some fun with me, and I appreciate it now, and I am thankful there was no actual quiz later.

As I was leaving his house, Rhon Wright told me that his son, David Wright, would be calling me soon. I was giddy at the thought of one of the best baseball players of the last 20 years, and an integral part of the book, would call me. A day or two later, I completed several interviews with parents, coaches, and mentors of the Splendid 6. My truck had a full tank from the local Wawa, and I was about to fill my stomach with an amazing Wawa Meatball Parm Hoagie. A 24-ounce coffee, Gatorade, and a so-called "Sharable" size of peanut M&Ms were beside me riding shotgun for the six-hour South Carolina drive from Hampton Roads. Traffic was at least triple what I remember during my brief time living in Hampton Roads as I tried to navigate tunnels and bridges to I-95 South and my eventual freedom to open my hoagie.

The truck's entertainment system fired up with a 757-area code number. I was sure it was someone I probably needed to talk to, but I was not expecting the person on the other end. "Hi, it's David Wright." I became a little flustered as I was stuck bumper-to-bumper and not able to really give him my best frame of mind without being distracted or dying in a slow-rolling fiery crash. I asked him if we could talk later, and he said sure, and to reach back when I had the time. At the next rest area, I texted David Wright back, apologizing for not being able to talk at that time. I was afraid he thought I was "Big-Timing" David Wright. Insert laugh soundtrack. Each hour I did not hear back accentuated my fear of missing my chance to talk to David Wright. Finally, around midnight, he texted back, and I was on Cloud Nine as we worked out over the next couple of days what to discuss on that Sunday afternoon. When the New York Giants knelt on back-to-back plays to allow better punt position, I hoped it was not an ominous sign for my call with David Wright shortly.

My worries shifted as David Wright began our conversation with fantasy football and the baffling New York Giants. After initially expressing his shock at New York and their alternative game planning, we began to talk about what we agreed to discuss: Towny Townsend and the Splendid 6. David Wright quickly gave much of the credit to Towny Townsend, but also the coach that Towny handed David Wright and his parents to, Coach Allan Erbe. I could quickly tell the lessons of his youth coaches stuck with David Wright; the person and a book really could happen.

As someone who retired from the Coast Guard and continued serving with Federal and State Service, I began to grow weary of not having a little more tactical control of my life as well as wanting to put more effective work into my always "this next audition is my breakthrough" Actor aspirations. I was able to convince my beautiful and patient wife that we should buy into the franchise of Maui Wowi Smoothies and Coffees and open an event and venue-based business. Flip-flops, a Hawaiian shirt, and a wheelbarrow to take all the money to the bank in was all I needed once we opened. All excited, we took the training classes, paid our franchise fees, and waited for our beautiful tiki hut bar. Then, literally the next week, the Covid-19 timeout was called and still clouds our TEAMMONTY event and venue-based career, but I have a staggering number of Hawaiian shirts in the closet.

Not discouraged, I took solace in baseball even more than usual. I read book after book about baseball, watched any game I could. Who knew Korean baseball was so fun to watch?

As Covid clouds begin to lift and normalcy is attempting to return, baseball is still standing, and I hope this book feeds your baseball soul. Please enjoy this book as much as I enjoyed writing it and getting to know some of the amazing people in it.

ONE:

THE TIDEWATER BASEBALL MIRACLE

I won't be happy until we have every boy in America between the ages of six and sixteen wearing a glove and swinging a bat.

–Babe Ruth

Love is, in many ways, a miracle of faith and hard work. Baseball was the same for Marvin "Towny" Townsend. If you have not heard of him, you are not alone.

Towny Townsend's belief in hard work, the unconventional, and the power of positive thinking shaped baseball not only in a small slice of baseball heaven but in what would become an amazing group of baseball players in the Major Leagues. Towny, coaches, parents, and mentors holding the same drive and values helped reshape baseball into a new form called "Towny Ball," putting fun and passion back into baseball.

Babe Ruth was a giant among men in life and especially in baseball. But unfortunately, the Babe never seemed to fully grow up before succumbing to cancer and leaving way too soon. Though not a formally educated man, Babe Ruth held a Ph.D. in baseball and perhaps philosophy.

Babe Ruth once explained how to hit home runs. *I swing big with everything I've got. I hit big, or I miss big. I like to live as big as I can.*

The Babe did precisely that and left baseball too soon. Towny took his big swings too, and helped to show the way for a whole new generation of ballplayers coming up in a small and often forgotten spot in the world of baseball and into baseball greatness.

To begin to know Towny, his beginning is not the start. To know Towny, we need to learn about those he believed in…the players, coaches, and friends he surrounded himself with. "Teammates" in life, as he called them. Like the Babe, Towny's life path was too short and stolen by cancer, but so many others are pushing forward where his path slowly faded away. For each other and Towny.

The Splendid 6, the Amazing Miracle Mets of Tidewater, Tidewater Boys, or the Wonderboys of Tidewater, no catchy name can capture the work, chance, and grace seen through the eyes of coaches like Towny, his teammates, parents, and the Splendid 6 themselves.

TWO:
BASEBALL FORGOTTEN AND REBORN

Every life lesson is on that baseball field.

– Goose Gossage, Hall of Fame baseball pitcher

The region of Tidewater, Virginia, now more commonly known as Hampton Roads, was an athletic hotbed of exceptional talent supplying D1 College programs and professional sports leagues across our nation and world.

Pro football Hall of Famers with roots in the region include Henry Jordan, Dwight Stephenson, Lawrence Taylor, Bruce Smith, Clarence "Ace" Parker, and Chris Hanburger. And no one can forget the one player, who may not be in the Hall of Fame, but electrified Hampton Roads before the NFL: Michael Vick. Dozens of impactful players from Hampton Roads have taken the NFL by storm: All-Pro, MVPs, Pro-Bowlers, and Super Bowl champions.

Nancy Lieberman, a pioneer in Women's Basketball, played college ball at Old Dominion University in Norfolk. Allen Iverson played in Newport News before joining the Basketball Hall of Fame.

Olympic medals from Hampton Roads athletes such as track and field athlete Francena McCorory and Gymnast Gabby Douglas could fully decorate and brighten a Christmas tree.

Athletes from Hampton Roads are enshrined in the NFL, NBA, Golf, and Boxing Hall of Fames. But Major League Baseball, the national pastime, held a seat in the corner often overlooked in Hampton Roads, until Towny's vision bought Hampton Roads into Major League Baseball's forefront and focus.

Baseball, before Towny, in Hampton Roads has a long history. Impactful, but not in players from the region being often selected for the Minor Leagues or playing in the Major Leagues. Baseball with Towny and his coaches influences baseball overflowing from the Coastal Virginia area to across America.

The attractions of Virginia and its lower peninsula, fertile land, navigable waterways, and other natural resources long attracted people. The first English settlers were in nearby Jamestown. Our nation's independence was formally earned on Yorktown and Civil War battlefields and near its ports and further offshore.

Hampton Roads is located in Southern Virginia, at the mouth of the James River, as it empties near the mouth of Chesapeake Bay. Hampton and Newport News lay to the north shore of the river, and Virginia Beach is 10 miles to the east on the coast of the Atlantic Ocean. These cities and Portsmouth, Chesapeake, and Norfolk for the Hampton Roads area, formerly known as the Tidewater area.

More than a dozen baseball teams and leagues set up in Tidewater since almost the beginning of professional baseball. Funny team names such as the Norfolk Clam Eaters, Norfolk Clams, and the Tars played in small stadiums across the area from the late 1800s until the 1950s, when the New York Yankees closed their Class B Piedmont League team.

The New York Yankees had a minor league team in Norfolk from 1934 until 1955, with many of its stars learning and growing under the eyes of the fans in the Hampton Roads region.

The actual New York Yankees even played against the Norfolk Tars in a 1934 exhibition game at a park known initially as League Park before the name Bain Field stuck. The game included Hall of Famers like Babe Ruth, who had four base hits; and Lou Gehrig was hit by a pitch scaring the crowd and the Yankees. Nevertheless, Lou Gehrig worked on his long-standing 2,130 Major League record of consecutive games played until Cal Ripken, Jr. broke the record decades later.

Christy Mathewson, part of Major League Baseball's Hall of Fame first class to be inducted in 1936, pitched for a team in Norfolk before taking his talent to the New York Giants and 373 National League wins. With their farm team for over 20 years, the New York Yankees graced the area with great baseball names to cheer for, including Yogi Berra, Phil Rizzuto, Whitey Ford, and Vic Raschi.

Phil Rizzuto hit .336 for the Piedmont League champion Tars in 1938. The "Scooter" played on Casey Stengel's Yankee dynasty in New York from 1941 to 1956. Rizzuto played shortstop for the Yankees, helping to win 11 American League pennants and 8 World Series. Rizzuto was finally voted into the Hall of Fame in 1994.

Vic Raschi struggled to a 4-10 pitching record for the Norfolk Tars in 1942. But Raschi won 20 or more games in a season for the Yankees three times and anchored the starting rotation in the 1940s and 1950s.

Yogi Berra showed what would be his specialty later with the New York Yankees by playing for the Piedmont League playoff championship Tars team in 1943. Berra played 18 years as a Hall of Fame Player and was a coach and manager for the New York Yankees, New York Mets, and Houston Astros. Berra played on 10 world championship teams. Berra managed the Yankees to the pennant in 1964 and bought the Mets to the National League championship in 1973. Berra was inducted into the Hall of Fame in 1972.

Whitey Ford, the great New York Yankees pitcher, played for the Norfolk Tars in 1948, finishing with a 16-8 record. Ford pitched on 10 pennant-winning teams, 5 of which won the World Series. Ford went 236-106, a .690 winning percentage, the second-highest all-time. Ford was inducted into the Baseball Hall of Fame in 1974 along with Mickey Mantle.

Hampton Roads has a rich baseball history, but is a military town, especially a U.S. Navy and U.S. Coast Guard town. Naval Station Norfolk is the largest naval complex globally, and the U.S. Coast Guard bases its Atlantic Area Operations out of Portsmouth. Close to 250,000 military veterans live in the Hampton Roads region. The military is a complexion of American society, and baseball is part of that. Baseball and softball fields are across military bases and are full of young men and women playing the game.

The U.S. Navy loved sports and baseball so much they built an all-purpose stadium in 1918 at Naval Station Norfolk. The stadium is now the second oldest continuously used brick baseball stadium in the United States. The oldest is Wrigley Field in Chicago for the Cubs. Like Wrigley Field, the stadium became the home baseball field for some of the game's all-time greats.

Many Major League players served their country on active duty. In addition, they played on the many local fields for service teams in the area during World War II, including Baseball Hall of Famer's Bob Feller, Pee Wee Reese, and Phil Rizzuto.

The field is now named McClure Field after Capt. Henry McClure, the Commanding Officer in Norfolk, who decided to hold a Navy World Series. The Bluejackets beat the Airmen in the "World Series" event only seen by the military in 1943.

The echoes of professional baseball faded in Hampton Roads as teams like the Norfolk Tars, Portsmouth Cubs, and the Portsmouth Merrimacs ceased operations in the area by 1955.

In 1961 baseball returned with the Portsmouth-Norfolk Tides. The team became the Tidewater Tides over time, and is the most prominent and lasting baseball team in the Hampton Roads area during the last 100 years.

The Tides formed in 1961 in the South Atlantic League and were non-affiliated with any Major League Baseball team before gaining a limited affiliation with the Kansas City Athletics. Since then, the Tides have been affiliated with the St. Louis Cardinals, Chicago White Sox, and Philadelphia Phillies.

An amazing year for the Miracle Mets was 1969. With former Norfolk Tars player Yogi Berra as a 1B coach, the New York Mets took home the World Series from the heavily favored Baltimore Orioles. But 1969 was an amazing year also for Hampton Roads. The New York Mets transferred their Triple-A affiliate from Jacksonville,

Florida to Hampton Roads, beginning a 38-year run in Hampton Roads before becoming the present-day Baltimore Orioles affiliate.

From 1969 to 2006 the Mets were able to put down a lot of roots and draw fan strength in the Hampton Roads community. A local Hampton Roads Baseball player even played for the Tidewater Mets before becoming one of the best players in franchise history and a team captain for the New York Mets. This player as a child often would come to games with his father and seek the autographs of the players He would indeed surpass one day and have the (W) right stuff to rewrite the Mets franchise record books.

THREE: BASEBALL BEGINNINGS

Hey Dad, wanna have a catch?
I'd like that.

– "Field of Dreams"

Baseball tends to be a game passed down to children from their fathers. Playing catch with "Dad" is both celebrated and mourned in the American consciousness and further instilled in movies like "Field of Dreams" or in songs like Harry Chapin's "Cat in the Cradle." Often a boy's or girl's first t-ball, softball, or baseball coach is one of their parents. These parents are "Rock Stars" and deserve appreciation and respect. Most of these parent coaches start their coaching journey as their child first shows interest and stop as they naturally gravitate to other sports or interests. Some of these children begin to outgrow the parents' coaching and need additional mentorship and coaching.

Passion, excellence, and attention to detail are traits needed to be a coach. So is a keen eye and the honesty to spot the right player who can be molded into a well-rounded scholar-athlete. The best of the best, just maybe, can compete for college scholarships, be signed as a free agent, or be drafted by a Major League Baseball organization.

The chances of playing college ball or being signed by a Major League organization are astronomically minimal. With each rising level, the funnel is narrowed to the baseball players. The competition is intense, and the love of the game and dedication must be instilled and held by the players.

To play in college or play in the major leagues is so far-fetched for kids it is almost criminal to think or verbalize it for them. Batting tees with the battle scars of glue and duct tape decorate millions of backyards and batting facilities as they are absolutely ravaged daily as bats muddle through a hitting zone the size of Texas. Thousands of hours are spent refining the contact zone of the baseball to 1/8th of an inch or less at a microsecond.

Parents' arms fall off as they throw grounders, line drives, and flyballs to their kids. The kids that fall in love with the ball often resort to various other methods to harness their skills and pass the time. A tennis ball against a wall, garage door, or stairs creates groundballs, line drives, and pop-ups. A broomstick or thin plastic bat hit rocks, bottle caps, tennis balls, or balls shaped out of whatever can be found; tape and rags are routinely used by baseball-crazed kids.

Home Run Derbys and two – or three-person wiffleball games with out of bounds laid down by a hat or a home run fence as the woodpile, are romanticized memories of childhood for many.

Movies are made like "Sandlot" on those feelings, and there is always a kid or even a parent running around baseball fields with a "You're Killing Me Smalls" T-shirt. However, some kids never quit regardless of skill; they just keep at it. A select few kids' skills are even able to be harnessed by such strange and unorthodox items as spinning and diving lid containers. Yes, lid containers. Cool Whip…

FOUR:
THE MAN, THE MYTH, THE TOWNY

Marvin "Towny" Townsend was born in Philadelphia on September 6, 1952. Towny's father was a Navy World War II, Korean, and a Vietnam veteran. Towny's father reached the rank of Master Chief, the highest enlisted rank in the Navy, over his 33 years of service. All the transfers and time his father deployed gave Towny and his older brother Jimmy the time to play baseball—lots of it. "He had a pretty rough childhood in some ways," said Cathy Townsend, Towny's widow.

Towny's father was a tough man, a man who knew how to fight, was quick to anger, and had a competitive mentality. Father to son is a pattern often repeated. However, both men mellowed as life moved forward. Towny's father worked on baseball with Towny as often as he could, and each time Towny would ask. But like many fathers, the lessons could be taught in a practicable, quick, and brutal fashion by today's standards. "His father taught him to hit the curveball by throwing it at him and hitting him in the face," explained Cathy Townsend.

Blair Townsend was a no-nonsense guy and that followed into baseball. He believed baseball was between the ears and did not overthink it. Years later, his grandson, Sean Townsend, as a 13-year-old, asked his grandfather about the relationship of feet and a baseball swing. Instead of a technical answer full of baseball jargon, Blair Townsend answered his grandson with a response as simple and effective as his preferred black coffee.

"I had a tough day at the plate, and I asked my grandfather; I am not sure what I am doing with my feet, stepping this way and my bailing out. My grandfather said, 'Son, I don't know how you can hit a baseball with your hands thinking about your feet because there is nothing with your feet that will help you get the barrel to the ball. It's your hands to the ball.'"

Like many, Towny's baseball journey began at home. His father, often with a cigarette in his mouth, would toss and spin bottlecap after bottlecap at Towny for hitting practice. Blair Townsend was a four-pack-a-day smoker. Either a cup of black coffee or cigarette always seemed to be in his hand, but he tried the best he could to be there for his children.

The spin, dart, and movement of a bottle cap spun from the hands of a skilled thrower and the minuscule size can frustrate and even anger the batter. But the cap can also teach concentration and help sharpen hitting skills. Bottlecaps for kids loving baseball are as old as bottlecaps and baseball itself.

Hitting a tossed bottlecap has a two-fold advantage. First, the pitcher builds arm strength and refinement of throwing motions. At the same time, the batter has to build the skills to react to the movement of cutting in, dipping, diving, and all sorts of other "Mariano Rivera"-like movements. The size of a bottlecap also makes the baseball appear huge and mentally easier to hit. If you are alone and would like a ball thrown and fielded against the wall, tossing the bottlecap straight up with your hand and then swinging at it can increase hand-to-eye coordination. It also teaches to stay back on the ball and allows "Bat Lag," keeping the bat and ball in the hitting-zone milliseconds longer.

Towny became so good at hitting bottlecaps that the actual baseball became easy and fun to hit. Towny was a storied high school baseball player in Norfolk and was asked to sign a minor league contract after high school. Towny wanted to sign as a youngster at 17, but his father wanted him to mature, and his mother wanted him to attend college. Towny, a loving and faithful son, abided by his father's wishes and didn't sign yet and understood his mother's wish to go to college.

Towny went on to play college baseball at the College of the Albemarle in North Carolina and Campbell University in North Carolina. Townsend was a two-time All-Conference player, earning All-Region, NAIA All-American, and third-team All-American by the American Association of College Baseball Coaches.

Perhaps an even more significant honor and a foreshadowing of his ability to inspire and lead others was being named the captain of 1972 and 1973 nationally ranked teams. Major League teams took notice and kept knocking, knocking, knocking, and knocking on the door for Townsend.

Townsend was first drafted by the California Angels in the second round of the 1973 January regular-phase MLB draft. Next, the Pittsburgh Pirates tried to get Towny with the fourth round of the 1973 MLB June-secondary-phase draft. Next, the Baltimore Orioles took a swing to get Towny to leave college ball at Campbell University, North Carolina, with the 22nd pick of the 1974 June amateur draft. When the Boston Red Sox took Towny with the 18th pick of the first round of 1974 MLB June secondary draft, Towny—a shortstop and third baseman—finally relented and signed a contract playing for the Boston Red Sox organization with a college degree nearly complete.

Towny's Minor League baseball journey began in 1974 at Winston-Salem in "A" ball at age 21. Unfortunately, like so many other marvelously gifted athletes, even those highly drafted and sought-after like Towny, a Minor League career is as far as it goes, and he fell short of the Major Leagues. Townsend's Minor League career spanned 1974 and 1975. Towny handled the left side of the infield at shortstop with third baseman Butch Hobson. Hobson went on a couple years later to hit 30 home runs and drive in over 100 for the Boston Red Sox in 1979.

Towny was fiercely loyal and protective of his family, and especially his mother. However, a sharp racist exchange by his own team's manager and his Italian mother ended up with Towny, borrowing from his father's Navy Boxing Champion skills and training, fracturing the manager's jaw. Fairly or not, the result was the end of Towny's Major League baseball dreams as the Boston Red Sox released him. Towny was a high-draft pick multiple times, but baseball back then was not nearly as forgiving as it is now for player indiscretions. As a result, no other team offered Towny a contract, and his professional baseball career came to a heartbreaking and sudden halt.

"Towny did not allow the injustice that happened to him as a player to stop his love of baseball. It allowed him to become a more balanced coach," said Gary Lavelle. "In today's game, with all the money-high draft picks, no way would that happen today, players would get more opportunities and teams now treat the players better," explained Gary Lavelle, longtime friend, and former MLB All-Star player.

Towny Townsend only did what many of us would have done in the same situation. Towny's situation happened to many players years before and in the years since. African American Baseball players like Jackie Robinson and Larry Doby, as the first players desegregating baseball, were warned not to fight back and take the insults hurled at them and around them.

Fighting back with physical violence, no matter if it is justified or not, can have career-ending repercussions, and it was a lesson Towny learned the hard way and didn't want his players to walk in those footsteps. A promising African American baseball high school player learned of the story the first time and was shocked that even a white man like Towny could face racist epithets in the South, and it stuck with him as he ascended the Minor Leagues and throughout his Major League career. Coach Townsend's lasting baseball lessons and knowledge of the game were so much more than his Minor League statistics would suggest as a player.

Seventy-eight base hits in 391 at-bats for a .200 Batting Average with 0 Home Runs and 32 Runs Batted In. The numbers were not what he wanted, but he had the gift of taking his professional baseball-playing journey as far as he could take it, making him a rare player sought after and drafted by four Major League teams. In addition, Towny was close to finishing his college degree that he promised his mother he would achieve.

Towny went back to playing baseball as he could as he was wrapping up his college degree. An adult amateur baseball league in Norfolk became a suitable outlet for competitiveness. Over the years, the people Towny would meet in the adult baseball league became part of his circle or, as his "Team." Towny was lucky enough to meet his future wife there as well.

FIVE:
THE BASEBALL WIFE

Even decades after meeting Towny, Cathy Townsend's eyes still grow brighter with a bit of sadness mixed in reminiscing about their first meeting and recounting their early days.

"I met Towny at a baseball game. He played in the Tidewater Summer League, mostly of adults and college students home for the summer. He had just been released from the Boston Red Sox and was finishing his bachelor's degree at Virginia Wesleyan College. I went to the game with a girlfriend whose boyfriend was the catcher on Towny's team. My friend told me there were 18 players on the field; pick one. I watched the players as they warmed up. Towny was tall, tanned, and olive-skinned as he was half-Italian. Muscular but slim. He was poetry in motion, and everything looked effortless. I picked him. He booted the ball when he took his last ground ball to come into the dugout. As he jogged towards the dugout, he looked up and raspberried me. Later he came out of the dugout and picked up some baseballs lying around, and started juggling them. We smiled at one another. After the game, Pam and I waited outside the locker room for her boyfriend to come out, and Towny came out before him. Steve had given Towny my phone number, unbeknownst to me. He took my hand and said, "My name is Towny," passing me. He had also put a piece of paper in my hand. After he walked away, I looked at the paper. It had his name and his phone number on it. He called me that same night," explained Cathy Townsend.

Although Towny had long hair and big 1970s side chops, Towny and Cathy began to date. A year of dating led to a 9-month engagement with marriage in 1978. Cathy and Townsend later welcomed two baseball-playing sons, Sean in 1981 and Chase in 1985. A family formed, and a nucleus of what would become part of his coaching legacy focused.

Cathy Townsend knew marriage to Towny Townsend would be crowded, with baseball as its mistress, or with Cathy as the mistress to baseball? It didn't matter to her, she just wanted to be with him, and she knew baseball was a huge part of his life. "I just knew baseball was going to be his first love, and I'd be second, and I was okay with that," said Cathy Townsend.

"Sometimes I did feel lonely at times, but he was willing to listen to me in his way. I asked him for a date night to spend more time together. He came home one night all excited and said we would have date night every Friday night. I was like, Wow, it's even more than I was hoping for. Then he told me he just signed us up for Co-Ed softball on Friday nights. We played for three years, and I truly enjoyed myself," said Cathy Townsend.

Towny always seemed comfortable around kids and sports. Helping to shape and build through sports and letting the kids have the fun and being lost in games as they should. Even before the Townsend children's birth, Towny was learning how to be a dad and a coach to a model youth sports organization.

"Towny was always involved with kids. When I met him, he was the director at the local Recreation Center. He ran tournaments there and helped with the kids there. He played baseball with them and basketball. Towny was always around kids, and he learned very quickly how to handle kids, and they loved him," explained Cathy Townsend.

Some people stick their heads in the sand instead of seeing and helping to make a difference for no other reason than it is right. Towny did what had to be done, for no other reason than if not him, than who? Towny often found himself in situations well beyond his position description as a teacher or youth coach, but well within the boundaries of himself of always answering the bell if others needed help.

"Towny was always driven to kids that needed help. There was a kid who had the same birthday as Towny. His dad was abusive to his mother. He was about 16, and he tried to get between his dad and his mom. His dad threatened to kill him. His mom told him to leave the house," said Cathy Townsend. "The kid called Towny from a payphone around midnight with no shoes on. Towny went and got him and kept him at the house for the weekend. "Just call your mom and tell her you are okay," Cathy said Towny told the boy.

His oldest son Sean remembers another time involving law enforcement and one of his former players needing a lifeline and still knowing he could count on Towny to be there if called upon.

Sometimes the help resulted in a good ending with a turnaround and others just being another fork in the path of poor decisions. But Towny was always ready to help in a time of need.

"One time, he woke me up at one or two in the morning, and we drove to Chesapeake jail. He looked at me on the drive and said, 'I got one shortstop in the Major Leagues and one in Chesapeake Jail.' He bailed him out, and the kid ended up running on the bail," said Sean Townsend. "This kid was in jail, and he would make one call, and it was to my dad because he knew my dad would come to get him," said Sean Townsend.

But for Towny Townsend, his role of father to Sean and Chase had to come first. Being the head coach of a team with your child on it can place a wedge of resentment between them, or the hours and commitments can cause the father to miss games of another child he should be at.

Towny put Sean and his baseball first. Sean said he wanted Towny to see more of his high school games as a senior; Towny stepped down from high school coaching that year and promised to make sure he was at all his games. "He didn't miss any," said Sean Townsend.

The actions of his father inspired Sean Townsend to afford his children the same opportunities he asked of his Father.

"When he did that, it gave me a different perspective, and later on in my life, I stepped down from high school coaching because I wanted to do the same for my kids," said Sean Townsend.

Towny could be a fan of Sean, but the Father-Son coaching dynamic was not always a good thing between Towny and Sean. "He would say "throw it harder" when I was pitching, and I would throw it slower on purpose, just to piss him off," said Sean Townsend sheepishly. The dynamic with Sean was different than with Chase. He coached Chase through high school. "If my dad had his hat on, it was "Coach," not "Dad," explained Chase Townsend on the dynamic of being a coach's son. And it worked for them.

After leaving the Minor Leagues, Towny began his first Coaching job at Virginia Wesleyan University, a small Division III program. Major league draft picks are seldomly generated at schools like that, but six players were drafted into the Major Leagues, and Towny won the Conference's Coach of the Year twice in the three years coaching there.

Towny Townsend and Matt Sinnen later became lifelong friends and fellow baseball coaches. But first, their relationship started with a promise Towny made him while recruiting Matt to become his first baseball recruit at Virginia Wesleyan. Sinnen excelled as a Catcher, setting the Career Batting average at Virginia Wesleyan with a .403 before being selected by the Pittsburgh Pirates in the 1980 June Amateur Draft.

"I have to say Towny is probably one of the three greatest mentors in my life next to my older brother John and my father. There weren't too many people knocking on my door, telling me if I did whatever he told me to do for three years, I'd get myself drafted. So, I did, and three years later, in 1980, I was drafted and played minor League Baseball," said Matt Sinnen.

Although he was no longer in Minor League Baseball, Towny still had some professional baseball strokes, allowing him to show his college players some of the perks of being a professional baseball player.

"I remember playing for Towny at Virginia Wesleyan college; how many Division Three teams get on a bus then go to Florida for spring training and play games down there?" said Matt Sinnen. "Towny took us there, and we saw Ted Williams and Carl Yastrzemski flipping balls to Towny because they knew Towny was on the outside looking in after that incident, and they understood it was wrong. Back in that day, there are a couple things you didn't do, you didn't gamble on baseball, and you certainly couldn't punch a manager in the face and play baseball again," said Matt Sinnen.

Elite athletes are wired differently. The drive to compete against themselves and others does not simply go away when the last whistle blows or out is recorded. Even as Towny was facing mortality, ferocity and competitiveness were still in high gear for him.

Even as Towny did get older, slowed down by cancer, his competitive streak remained as fiery as ever. Towny's children would not escape the brunt of it occasionally or witness it.

"My Father was an incredibly intense person. As a senior in high school, my father was throwing batting practice; he was at least 50 and had cancer already. He threw it in about letter-high, and I hit it out further than I ever hit one before. The next time I came up, he drilled me in the back of the head," said Chase Townsend.

His son Sean Townsend tells of another time when most dads would have declined to participate in a sporting event, but the competitive juices were still flowing the last year of his life.

"A year before he died, I was in a softball league. He came out because we were a player short. At this point, he had half of his tongue removed, with pieces of his arm and leg cut out to repair it. He played second base. He went 3-3, dislocated his shoulder running to first base, and popped it back in," said Sean Townsend. Cathy Townsend had seen enough and pulled the plug on Towny. "My mom stepped in and said, 'That's it, you're done.' My father turned to the team and apologized for letting the team down. But, like really, 3 hits in 3 at-bats, with one arm, 53, dying of cancer, and still the best player on the field. He died less than a year later," said Sean Townsend.

Towny Townsend did not lack intensity and focus. He first introduced himself to what would become a lifelong friend and the future Co-Founder for the main rival to his Blasters, Gary Wright of the Drillers, with a reminder of baseball's unwritten rules.

Like many people to enter Towny's life, Gary Wright entered through baseball. "I never knew Towny before; he was on the mound pitching, Towny could throw hard, 92 to 94 MPH," explained Gary Wright. "Maybe I was crowding the plate, I am not sure. But Towny placed a fastball right into the middle of my back. I just kind of stood there for a few seconds. It really hurt. Towny yelled at me to take my base. Matt Sinnen, his catcher, and former player of his from Virginia Wesleyan, encouraged me to take my base as well. I was pretty mad," said Gary Wright. "My next at-bat I turned on his pitch and drilled it for a home run. I proceeded to look at it and take a slow home-run trot. Towny threw his glove down in anger and ran up to meet me at the plate. As I rounded third base and saw Towny and Matt standing there with a whole lot of muscle just waiting for me, I knew I was about to get a beat-down. I got it, that's for sure," laughed Gary Wright.

Towny's competitive streak never waned. "It was remarkable. Even as he hit his 40s, he was still bringing it. We would go to Kings Dominion every year for fun. They had a radar gun to measure your fastball and then post it on the leaderboard. He would spend 25 or 30 bucks warming up because he was going to go for it and air it all out each time," said Sean Townsend. "Sometimes, he would warm up in the parking lot and then walk into Kings Dominion to throw for the speed gun. It was funny to go to a theme park and straight to the pitching game just to see if you can be the highest velocity recorded for the summer," explained Sean Townsend. "While we were walking around the park, he had to keep passing by it to see if anybody threw one harder. Then, he would proceed to throw again," said Cathy Townsend. "One night, he wore his arm out because some 18 – or 19-year-old high school kid was bringing it and knocking him off the top spot. He was probably in his mid-40s but going dollar-to-dollar and throw-for-throw with the kid," laughed Chase Townsend.

That determination and competitiveness shined through when Towny was pushing into his mid-40s and challenging an 18-year-old who later competed in an All-Star Game Home Run Derby with the Major League's most prolific sluggers. An 18-year-old Michael Cuddyer, recently selected as a first-round pick who would become an All-Star MLB player would surely give Towny Townsend a tougher battle than some kid at an amusement park.

"Mike Cuddyer and Towny had a Home Run derby between the two of them. Mike was probably 18 because he was just getting ready to go into pro ball. I think the challenge came from the kids at the camp. Towny said, 'Let's go kid; let's have a home run challenge.' Michael said, 'aren't you too old?' Towny shot back, 'Ok, let's go,'" said Cathy Townsend. She was proud as she went on to describe how Towny ended up beating Michael Cuddyer. But did a coach older than the oldest of Major League players at that time really believe he would beat the first round baseball pick poised for All-Star Games and a batting title? "Yeah, absolutely," laughed Cathy Townsend.

According to Cathy Townsend, Michael Cuddyer was not disappointed or even surprised at the baseball skills Coach Towny Townsend broke out and how proud Towny was to beat the up-and-coming Major League baseball star.

When I tried to remind him of the story or raise the remote possibility he let the "old man" win, Michael Cuddyer, now approximately Towny's age at the time of the derby, claims to not remember the incident. But I think I saw the softest wink as he feigned a memory gap as we sipped coffee.

Coaching in Division III baseball is often not prosperous. However, some further stability was acquired for Coach Townsend, so he earned a master's degree and began a career in Money Management. Towny thought about trying to get a baseball job as an Assistant Coach at the NCAA D1 level, and maybe even trying to kick the tires to try to play professionally as the Los Angeles Angels showed an interest, but Towny felt his best version of himself would be back to his roots.

SIX:
TOWNY AND HIS EXTRAORDINARY TEAMMATES

Coach Townsend had his guys, his teammates in life, and an extraordinary group of coaches, including Allan Erbe, Manny Upton, Gary Lavelle, Matt Sinnen, Gary Wright, and a Major League Baseball local scout, Billy Swoope. All these coaches took a different journey to the same place, converging in Hampton Roads during the 1990s to make—even just for a moment—the most formidable youth team in any sport at any time.

No Little League World Series team had the amount of talent to later flood colleges, the Minor Leagues, Major Leagues, and even Major League All-Star teams the way the Splendid 6 of Tidewater did. Even the Fab-5 of Michigan couldn't make the lasting impact on their sport of basketball the way the Splendid 6 helped shape baseball during the first and second decades of the 21st Century.

All these coaches had to come together, like a perfect chaos, at the right time and right way to make the baseball world stop and take notice of the amazing players the once sleepy baseball fields of Hampton Roads churned out. How did it happen? Towny Townsend, vision, and his friends and coaches all shared a common and consistent belief in helping to further develop the kid into a better person, often resulting in making a better player too, which became the more important of the two.

Around the time Towny's baseball career and personal life shifted, Gary Lavelle made his debut as a pitcher for the San Francisco Giants. His Minor League journey was different than Towny's. He was a 20th-round pick out of Bethlehem Liberty High School in Bethlehem, Pennsylvania. From 1967 through 1974, Lavelle played in towns like Medford, Oregon; Decatur, Georgia; and Amarillo, Texas, across seven Minor League baseball seasons.

Lavelle knew and felt each mile of the long journey from the Minor Leagues to the Major Leagues. A Minor League baseball life is low pay, long hours, bad food, no privacy, and not made for all baseball prospects. Long bus rides across our long dusty and hot highways can quickly turn into pushing through heavy rains and whipping winds. Nevertheless, after retiring as a player, Lavelle came back decades later to ride the buses again, this time as a Minor League pitching coach for the New York Yankees and their Double-A team in Trenton, New Jersey. Lavelle is the epitome of a baseball Man.

Lavelle was primarily a starting pitcher in the Minor Leagues before pitching out of the bullpen for the 1974 San Francisco Giants. Lavelle excelled so long and often out of the bullpen that he set the games pitched record for the long-tenured and storied franchise. He is in the San Francisco Giants Hall of Fame after retiring from his 13-year Major league career, making the All-Star team twice.

Coach Lee Banks became the beneficiary of these great players when he assembled the team featuring some of the players that would make Hampton Roads a mandatory stop for college and Major League scouts. Lee Banks is still a force to be reckoned with in baseball circles, with his knowledge and uncanny sense of keeping a team in harmony.

As a coaching prodigy, Towny Townsend is worthy of being in any conversation of a manager or coach, including Casey Stengel, Sparky Anderson, Bill Belichick, or Vince Lombardi. Coaches and managers develop players and surround themselves with coaches who augment and amplify the best for the team. The roots and limbs of coaching trees resonate for years to come.

These coaches each held a different specialty. Towny was spinning tops to mimic cutters, curves, and breaking balls. Lavelle would occasionally coach with the team but was always there to make kids love the game, show the importance of accuracy, and spin the ball from the mound. Coach Manny Upton possessed skills and knowledge in many sports, and his optimism was contagious. And of course, there was Coach Erbe with his no batting practice but an all-defense approach mentality.

"The coaches were a diverse bunch of characters," said Chase Townsend. The amount of knowledge and experience the coaches possessed was staggering, but is a child born to be a great baseball player needing to be polished by instruction, or is it genuinely developed with parameters of patience and hard work of the player, coaches, and those that love them?

The answer may turn out to be both, despite Coach Erbe's humble and gracious mindset on the question.

Coach Erbe, who coached David Wright with the Blasters, may not believe his coaching helped David Wright be a Major Leaguer. "My Mother could've coached David Wright, and he would still be a Major Leaguer. I'm prouder of some of the less talented players who went on to play ball in college and earn a degree," explained Erbe. "But I do think I helped him be prepared for the following levels of baseball," said Erbe.

SEVEN:

A BASEBALL CROWN PRINCE

Coach Allan Erbe is a unique person and a forward-thinking baseball coach with a bookcase of baseball history at home. The ever-brewing storm of Coach Erbe is parts historian, analytics creator, motivator, comedian, ball-buster with a dash of the free spirit of a hippie, but 100% baseball man.

Coach Allan Erbe was an excellent coach with Towny and the Blasters. Friends with baseball experience and a strong respect between the two baseball men. Would Coach Erbe be the coach he was without Coach Towny Townsend? Would Towny Townsend have been the coach he was without coaches around him like Coach Allan Erbe? It does not matter. It just worked.

Coach Erbe and Coach Townsend first met, as many baseball players do. The baseball diamond was their first connection and continued to be as the two bonded throughout their lives.

"I played against him back in the Norfolk Adult Summer Baseball League, so we kind of knew of each other," explained Erbe. "I first met him through John Dannemann, who played at the University of North Carolina as a left-handed pitcher and was drafted by the Montreal Expos. Dannemann was on my team, and he was friends with Towny. I lived with Dannemann in some apartments in Virginia Beach, and Towny would come over. So, we just kind of hit it off, and then we played together on his adult team," explained Erbe.

People genuinely knowing and loving baseball can spot each across a baseball field or even within a few minutes of routine conversation. The coaching styles may have been slightly different to the naked eye, but both coaches held the same overall goals bred on practice, repetition, and an underlying focus of respect and love for the team and sport.

"Towny did many repetitions, jingles, slogans, and drills. I was a little more cerebral, but I did a lot of repetition. Sometimes, I would spend two hours on a single thing like a first and third defense at practice," explained Erbe. "I figured that's the only way they're going to learn it was one thing at a time. So, I didn't want to throw eight or nine things at them at one practice. But both of us required the players to work hard, and we were pretty hard ass at discipline," said Erbe.

Allan Erbe tended to coach like a college professor. "He wanted to give kids baseball smarts, and most of the parents didn't know any better, so we wanted batting practice a lot. But Al always wanted fielding practice," said Rhon Wright.

"Al would be talking how and where to be in various situations, knowing this and that when you get into a rundown, find somebody to run into, he would come up with these nuanced things and teach the kids. When David started playing professionally, he knew scenarios and what to do before many of his teammates were first taught. David called and said what Coach Erbe taught worked brilliantly, and some of the coaches complimented him on his advanced baseball knowledge," said Rhon Wright.

Coach Allan Erbe looks and sounds like he would be more at home with a tropical shirt and a cold drink in his hand on a deck or a beach. But don't let that persona fool you. His baseball mind is cerebral, deliberate, elaborate, and competitive. Erbe is a blend of an old-school baseball coach and sports psychologist. Players were not just coached to field, hit, and run; they were taught the game's finer points and shown how to visualize their success. Unfortunately, not every player parent is conducive for such a way of thinking, and Coach Erbe split the parents into two different camps in his perspective.

"I noticed in the whole process there are two types of parents: those who say my kids are the 'greatest thing in the world' and the 'tough on him' parents," explained Coach Erbe. "When a player comes home and says he is not starting, the parent can either say the kid should be starting, placing blame on the coaches; or ask the child if he is playing his best and needs to play better? Those were David Wright's parents," Erbe said.

Trusting the team building and playing time were taught early and were something the kids and parents would have to learn to usually achieve the next level of their baseball goals. "One day, I made a list of all the kids that quit baseball, didn't play in college, and even in high school. The parents of those players were the kind of parents that would enable their children instead of pushing them," explained Erbe. "We had a few kids go to other teams over playing time. One parent had a lot of money, and he started his own team and batted his kid third. It was 'Daddy Ball,' which was fine for them," said Erbe.

But Daddy Ball was not for Coaches like Townsend, Erbe, Sinnen, and Wright.

Coach Erbe never cut a player once they made his team. He had a "develop the player" mentality with not just trying to compile an All-Star team, but players with the grit and potential to work and be better and possibly be prepared for teams in their baseball future. But missteps and challenges to team chemistry and philosophy are bound to happen. Occasionally parents and player assessments are not aligned with a coach's view.

"One of the mistakes I may have made was taking on some kids that the players and parents were better suited for "Daddy Ball," explained Erbe. "I was always upfront with their parents, I think he's got potential; he's not ready to play every day with us now, but we can help him make him better," said Erbe. "We had one father, we would have meetings with the parents after every practice, and during the Winter into Spring, we'd have individual sit-downs with the parents to tell them the strengths and weaknesses of their player and where they stood with the team. The father I was talking about said his son was in our top-three players along with David Wright and B.J. Upton. I'm never speechless, but he was number 13 out of 13," said Erbe.

According to Coach Erbe, those types of parents—the ones not able to see the child for the player they are and not pushing the player to face challenges and work harder for what is wanted—are the ones to not really make their next level in their baseball endeavors.

A well-rounded baseball education was a specialty and expected within the Blaster's organization. Coach Erbe used to photocopy players' baseball cards, displaying the picture-perfect form of what got them to the Major Leagues as teaching points and tucked into his continually growing coaching notebooks.

Like a baseball John Madden, he would draw up baseball plays for the 11 - and 12-year-olds. But then, it was defense and more defense, five-man infields, pick-off plays, and bunt defenses. His practices would not have an established time limit. And even after the athletic practice on the field ended, they would often sit for 30 to 45 minutes to discuss the finer points of baseball defense.

Years later, David Wright learned the same finer points in the minor leagues that Coach Erbe pounded into the players' heads. "It was crucial, and I felt it gave me an edge," said David Wright.

Coach Erbe spent as much time on the defense and mental aspects of the game. Coach Erbe even used visualization techniques to strengthen the players. "Having David Wright out there was like having an extra coach out there. He was that smart as a ballplayer," said Coach Allan Erbe.

The team went 189-71. At one point or another, Coach Erbe had on his 1995–1999 Blaster AAU team:

- Jason Moody: Played college ball at Christopher Newport University.
- Sean Slaughter: Played college ball at UNC-Greensboro and Internationally in Israel.
- David Marques: Academic Scholarship at Notre Dame.

- Vince Sibal: James Madison University and Virginia Tech.
- Eliot Erbe: Scholarship to Virginia Military University.
- Jeff DeMara: Scholarship to Virginia Military University.
- David Wright: First-Round pick for Mets in 2001.
- B.J. Upton: First-Round Pick by Tampa Bay Rays in 2002.
- Justin Upton: Team Bat Boy. No.1 Pick in 2003 by Arizona Diamondbacks.
- Josh Rupe: Third-Round pick by Chicago White Sox.
- Justin Orenduff: First-Round pick by Los Angeles Dodgers in 2004.
- Jacob Dempsey: 21st-Round pick by Philadelphia Phillies.
- Colin Roberson: 21st-Round pick by Florida Marlins in 2005.
- Matt Smith: Played five years in Minor Leagues for Texas Rangers and New York Mets.

Nine of the above went on to play professional baseball, with four being Fist-Round picks and two making Major League All-Star Games.

"Our teams were often undersized; one time a coach made a comment about the small stature of our pitcher, Jeff DeMara. I said, 'Don't worry, he gets taller when he pitches,'" laughed Coach Alan Erbe.

Coach Erbe is a core outstanding baseball man who helped establish the Hampton Roads area as a great baseball developmental juggernaut and a hotbed of big-league talent. Coach Erbe has continued to develop players and advance the baseball careers of local players over the last 35 years and still going.

EIGHT:
GIVING BACK

If you profess to love Baseball, you've got to give something back.

– Towny Townsend

The baseball passion never left Townsend as he returned to his alma mater, Lake Taylor High School in Virginia, and coached baseball. Spoiler alert: Coach Townsend took a historically urban and neglected baseball program in shambles and built a perianal winner.

"Towny Townsend went back to Lake Taylor High School to watch a game. The Lake Taylor kids came out dragging their feet, shirttails hanging out, long hair, cap sideways. Towny was appalled. He went to the principal and said, "You need a baseball coach, and I want to be your baseball coach," said Cathy Townsend.

Perhaps not entirely knowing what he had in front of him, the principal challenged back that he had to be a teacher in the school system. Towny had his Master's in Education as well as his student teaching. The principal took the win and Lake Taylor now had a new Physical Education Coach and a Driver's Education Instructor. More importantly, a coach and mentor willing to teach baseball and life to these kids, who were often overlooked and passed over.

"It was his calling to fix the program. No matter the talent level, any player had to hit the road if they were not interested in playing baseball the right way. The players that stayed respected Towny for it as they cut their hair, tucked in their jerseys, and wore the hat the right way. Towny believed in a clean-cut uniform, clean-cut everything, and good hard practice. The boys enjoyed the practice, and they enjoyed being with him," said Cathy Townsend.

Towny Townsend was the hometown baseball player big-shot coming home to coach his Alma Mater. The record of the Lake Taylor High School baseball team was 3-48 the previous three seasons and improved to 101-39 over the next eight seasons.

"Many of them didn't have dads or role models, so they kind of latched onto him. Also, the Norfolk High School demographic was a little more urban than the other schools in the area. So Towny tended to feel more comfortable in that kind of environment instead of the upper. He felt comfortable no matter where he was or with. Towny had a soft spot for the underprivileged kids; that's why he ran the MLB RBI Program in the Lake Taylor area for eight years before he passed away," explained Cathy Townsend.

Towny Townsend wanted to teach kids. It didn't matter how, where, or when. The underdog seemed to be Towny Townsend's favorite, and he could turn them into winners.

"Coach 'T' coached at a predominantly black school; they were good like you know killer-good. They came to play every time you played them. He knew there was talent there, and it was just nobody would teach them; Coach "T" did, though," said B.J. Upton.

NINE:

BLASTERS AND DRILLERS

Baseball players want to play baseball as long as possible and not just coach. Men's League baseball is an outlet for people who love baseball and once played on various levels to compete at a different and more challenging level than the slow-pitch softball teams. Other teams and sports leagues most approaching middle-aged men play. It was more baseball for Towny as he not just played on a team as when he met his wife but was looking for more.

The Drillers and then the Blasters were the adult baseball teams he played on, and Allan Erbe was a first baseman; Gary Wright and Melvin "Manny" Upton and Matt Sinnen were also on the team. Gary Lavelle was the pitcher. All of them, except Lavelle, had kids playing baseball. Upton had two young budding baseball players as sons who would one day put professional baseball scouts into a frenzy.

Coach Townsend and his friends in the adult baseball league had a problem seeing a baseball future for their kids at the local baseball fields.

Hampton Roads had so many great athletes but not enough high-level baseball levels to keep the players competing for higher-level baseball teams. In addition, the eastern side of Norfolk toward Virginia Beach was exploding with population, bringing more kids and needing more sports and options.

Of course, football and basketball were always well represented in colleges and professional leagues for young athletes of Hampton Roads with their long and demonstrated track record for producing not only NFL and NBA players but Hall of Fame quality players.

"For these baseball players to make it from a primarily a football and basketball area as well as a place with nowhere to play from to November to February, it is unbelievable for those guys to do it," said Manny Upton.

Local youth leagues competed from a young age. Still, not many games were played, and they often lacked the intensity and duration of baseball practice to advance their games past a rudimentary level. Coach Townsend could see a pocket of players needing more from baseball and coaching. Youth and Little League were simply not enough to bring consistent results and year-round competition. The traditional Little League, Pony, and Recreation Youth Leagues were short, only lasting a few months. Often an end-of-season All-Star team would compete, but the talent levels would often be diluted and ineffective with an extremely short supplement to their competitive season.

In short, an infrastructure was needed to produce a year-round program to practice in all weathers to keep pace with the players from warm weather and traditional hotbeds of baseball talent like Florida, California, and Texas. And Towny, his coaches, and the players who signed up for the upcoming ride had to pay the price. As a result, some friendships were broken, and some young players took the brunt of it. “I was kicked off my rec team and not allowed to play for two years because I missed All-Stars for an AAU Tournament,” said Chase Townsend.

Towny and his teammates had an answer: To create the higher level of baseball, with players he saw topping out the local Recreational and Little League teams and players from his baseball Day Camps that he often ran with Gary Lavelle.

“My Dad was not without his detractors. A lot of people back then associated with Great Bridge baseball did not like him for starting his teams,” said Sean Townsend. “It seems like American Legion and Rec Baseball dug in their heels, when there was plenty of room for everybody,” said Sean Townsend. “Ultimately, they both suffered because our AAU teams were a better product,” explained Sean Townsend.

A plan was hatched for the sake of not just for their kids but for kids and parents looking for something more, and the results were felt across professional baseball for decades. The Blasters were also going to start an AAU youth travel baseball team. In time the Drillers would, too.

Towny would classify the teams and organization as the answer for the good player who wants to get better. Towny reasoned there was no program for higher advanced kids who really loved the game and needed AAU Travel Baseball like the Blasters were able later to provide. Towny would not poach and convince players to play travel baseball. It was often the other way around, as Towny, and the Blasters, would often receive recommendations from coaches of players or their parents possibly ready for the Blasters. The Blasters, as an organization, was looking not just for playing ability but also the right mixture of attitude, coachability, and desire.

"For many of the players on those teams, it was their first taste of being in a truly competitive and developmental baseball environment," explained Erbe. "Towny was very competitive, more competitive than me. I was a little easier going. Towny was a little bit more driven, but we both were into developing the kids," said Erbe. "I think our coaching basic tenets were the same, and that is why he picked me to coach in his Blasters organization. The great thing about him is he was the leader of the organization, but he would not micromanage," explained Erbe.

"The coaches had the autonomy to run their teams with non-negotiable items such as 'don't embarrass the organization,' and your kids need to do well in the classroom. We did not want extra-curricular issues or shenanigans," said Sean Townsend.

On top of being the heart and soul of the Blasters, Towny was also the person scouring any ballfield he could to spot talent. "My father would identify talent and stockpile the organization. He ran the largest camps in this area for the longest time. At one point, we had 100 kids one week and then 100 kids the next. He had a day and a night session also. So, the team I was on was almost entirely born out of the camps," said Chase Townsend.

"Towny was the organizer, the one who started it all and then generally oversaw it. As I understood it as a parent, the coaches made decisions on their roster, but Towny had the final say. So, the direction that the organization would go went through him, and then he generally left each team up to the respective coaches," said Rhon Wright.

Towny had an eye for talent. But he was not just about picking players and trying to make them players they would not or could not become. Each player had a skill set he could see waiting to be unlocked or built on. Much like in basketball, the best coach would not turn Allen Iverson into a 7-footer in the paint, and David Wright could not be made into a Rickey Henderson and coached into stealing 130 bases in a season. David Wright had adequate to plus speed for his position and even stole 30 bases in a Major League season because he learned and was coached on how to play to the top of his skills and abilities.

"Towny organized these various age-level teams, and David was on one of them. Another son of ours, Stephen, played with Chase Townsend on a team Towny coached. I always thought Towny wanted to develop the kids, to bring out the best in them. If the name of your game was power hitting, he would work on that. He never tried to make Stephen into a David. Stephen was a fast and the top of the order hitter and a slap the other way. Towny never tried to turn him into a power hitter but worked with what Stephen had," said Rhon Wright.

To Towny, baseball could be a tool to help you with life skills. Baseball and its construct, the community around it, and the mentoring of caring individuals could shift and shape players and the person. "Towny wanted to develop the kids and teach life lessons through baseball. When we first met him, he was the Head Coach at Lake Taylor High School. If you're familiar with Norfolk, you know it's an urban community, and some of the kids playing for him came from some of the lower-income neighborhoods. Baseball was not a real popular sport there. The popular sports were football and basketball," said Rhon Wright. "Towny would get the kids to come out there, and he would work with them. Lake Taylor High School would routinely win district titles and occasionally run in the region. Towny knew how to see the kid, see his strengths and weaknesses, and try to build on them. In general, help the kid work toward being a better all-around kid. If the kid was good at baseball, that was a plus, but generally, he just wanted to develop the kid and make him a better person," said Rhon Wright.

It wasn't just Towny instilling lessons and values into the kids. Once David moved to Coach Allan Elbe's team, he was about to receive a somewhat different but valuable education.

"He just he loves the game, and he's a baseball rat. And there's zero chance I have the success I had in Baseball without a foundation. I mean, there's no doubt that I had such a leg up on everybody else going into high school and pro ball because of the foundation that you know that started with Towny, Gary Lavelle, and Coach Erbe. You couldn't ask for better teachers and mentors at a young age than what they gave me," said David Wright.

Towny believed there was more to being a Blaster than playing on the field, and he demanded more from each player. In Towny's own words from discussing his approach, "Most of them are used to being the star of their team. And here they are, just one player. I think it gives them a good perspective about life. These kids would play 24 hours a day if we asked. But there is more to this program than just playing baseball."

The Blasters baseball organization had a modest beginning as an AAU organization started with just one team, intending to develop the kids into good players and better human beings in a year-round setting with coaches and players being accountable to each other. The kids were often split up into two teams, a Red team and a White team. Baseball is a great game, but not all that much fun to practice over and over.

The Blasters played and practiced each other, playing whatever Youth League and Little League teams would agree to play or whatever event they could get into. It wasn't enough. The Boston Red Sox needed the New York Yankees to get better, and the Blasters required a team of equal skills to compete against and grow. "The Blasters needed a rabbit to chase," said Sean Townsend, Towny's son, an original member of the Blasters.

Coach Townsend turned to the now-older college recruit he once made good on a promise to. Sometimes intent and purpose are shifted through serendipity and fate to something even more significant and more extraordinary than initially intended. Townsend, perhaps with a stroke of luck or divine intervention, smoked a shot down the line appearing to be a foul ball before an unexplained gush of wind wrapped the ball for a home run around Fenway's Pesky's Pole. The unexpected can happen in baseball and was about to happen again.

"I went to a meeting to listen to Towny talk to prospective parents of the team. Towny wanted me to come coach for the Blasters. Everything sounded great. I said yeah, I love it, Towny, but let me think about it," said Matt Sinnen. "Towny looked at me and said, "Matt, if you profess to love baseball, you've got to give something back," said Matt Sinnen. "I thought about it and gave Towny a call the next day, and said, Towny, you are 100% right, and I do need to give back, but I think Gary (Wright) and I are going to start our own organization." And like that, a rabbit had two baseball organizations chasing it down.

Now Towny and the Blasters were genuinely ready to lift-off. Coach Gary Wright and Coach Matt Sinnen created separate teams, allowing two fully developed baseball organizations with similar year-round goals to square off. The Drillers arrived. The Blasters and Drillers began a competitive, bitterly fought, but always good-old-fashioned baseball rivalry with love.

For years, B.J. Upton took part in the Blasters and Drillers rivalry and compares it to the most intense of intense rivalries he has ever seen from a fan or player standpoint.

"It was Florida State versus Florida, Red Sox versus Yankees. Every time we played the Drillers, we wanted to beat them. So, there are no questions about it, Browns-Steelers. It's every rival you can think of. All the way from coaches, players, and all the way down to the parents," explained B.J. Upton.

The Blasters and Drillers never had a moment like the Red Sox and Yankees with Graig Nettles throwing down Bill "Spaceman" Lee or Pedro Martinez rolling Don Zimmer across the field. Still, each game was tightly contested, with both teams going hard for a win and bragging rights in the area. B.J. Upton still holds the Blaster pride close to his heart, but with a grudging respect for the Drillers' challenging games against them.

"We were better than the Drillers, but it was always a tight game with never any blowouts. I knew it was going to be a one – or two-run game every time and come down to the last six outs," said B.J. Upton. Justin Upton was a little younger than B.J., but still felt the same energy and rivalry.

The Blasters and Drillers were intense competitors as organizations and teams, but usually with a deep respect for each other and their methods. Sometimes the coaching philosophy of the coach of teams would clash across the baseball diamond. Coach Allan Erbe of the Blasters, and Coach Tyree Brown of the Drillers, were like oil and water on sportsmanship and how to use their players. Erbe was about the player at the position or order to ensure the best result for the team. Coach Brown may not have been as much.

Mark Reynolds first started with the Blasters and then finished as a Driller after his family moved and made the Drillers closer to the house for practices. Mark Reynolds and his parents saw the difference with the Blasters and Drillers with Coach Brown at the helm.

"Tyree Brown coached more with fear than encouragement. He was tough to play for," said Mark Reynolds.

Mark Reynolds' view from a player's perspective was not much different than Coach Erbe's. "Tyree Brown was a real jerk. He played his son at second base ahead of a kid named Colin Robertson, who got drafted by the Miami Marlins," explained Erbe. "I had a competition with everybody I coached against, but I wanted to beat him because he was a jerk, and I wanted to beat him worse than anybody else," said Erbe. "He was the bad sport. He wouldn't shake hands after games. We won the state championship against them one year, and he left before the trophy ceremony. A couple of his parents were so embarrassed, they went out and represented their team at the ceremony," said Erbe.

The way teams and players interact at tournaments for the week or weekend has a family trip or vacation dynamic. Time off for the family and vacation were often blended around those games.

"I don't think any of the parents liked him because he was very regimented. He wouldn't let the kids do anything on trips. Every year we'd go to the nationals, all these parents, that would be the family's vacation. It cost the families a lot of money to go," explained Erbe.

"One year we went to Minnesota, and they had the Mall of America indoor mall, that was our 12 and under team. I told the parents to get a room and take care of their kids. Brown would have curfews and team meals they had to go to each night, taking time away from the family. I just wanted the parents to ensure the players had a proper sleep," explained Erbe.

Brown's time with the Driller's organization was only three or four years and ended about as well as any game he lost to Coach Erbe and the Blasters. Coach Tyree Brown appeared to not have many of the same philosophies on building the person, player, and team as Coaches like Towny, Erbe, Sinnen, and Gary Wright.

"It was a friendly rivalry, but we didn't like them, and they didn't like us. The Drillers were good, but the Blasters were really good. We were trying to prove to them we were the better team. It was just a friendly competition; we knew we were better than the Drillers," explained Justin Upton.

The Blasters and Drillers Youth Baseball teams were born and raised through most of the coaches of the two organizations who competed against each other for many years in the local Adult Baseball League. As competitive as they were as players against each other, it was the same for coaches.

"My dad and all those guys all played the adult league for and against each other. So, it is how this whole thing even started. "Once the Drillers joined up, it was like "here we go," and there were flashes of the adult league sometimes," said B.J. Upton.

Not everything was rainbows and cotton candy from some baseball actions and behavior embedded from Towny to Matt Sinnen.

"Towny was certainly instrumental for me in my approach to baseball, and not all of that was fantastic. I remember that I probably got thrown out of too many kids' ball games because I wanted to be Towny. He was such a fiery guy," said Matt Sinnen. But Towny seemed to be a markedly changed man when he was a youth coach. "Towny certainly became a different human being the last 10 or 15 years of his life. By the time he was pushing the youth, it was a different kind of demeanor than before," explained Matt Sinnen.

Towny and his teammates' coaching styles, statistical analysis, and mental side were cutting edge back in the 1990s. Still, it was just foreshadowing where baseball evolved two decades later, starting in the 2010s.

"Toward the end of my career, everybody started getting mental skills coaches, and again these guys were mental skills coaches before there was such a thing. Especially with Coach Erbe giving us report cards with different numbers on them like old-school scout grading, circling different stats to improve, or what you were good at," said David Wright.

The term "forward leaning" describes what was being done with the Blasters and Drillers at the time and would have fit in well with Billy Beane and the Oakland A's during the 1990s.

"We had analytics departments and mental skills coaches before it was the in-vogue thing and before Major League Baseball did so. They were well ahead of their time regarding what they were teaching. We were the beneficiaries of it," said David Wright.

Towny Townsend was the proud "Godfather" of it all as the newly created AAU teams took off chasing each other across the baseball diamonds. Players from those teams would end up pursuing, competing, and pushing each other for decades across the country in College, Minor, and Major League Stadiums. World Championships were won, All-Star Teams made, and Major League records were broken by these players. Towny and the other coaches were going to provide kids an education in life and baseball.

Coach Allan Erbe still carries on his tradition of mailing envelopes and boxes to David Wright and other players containing information, pictures, and baseball observations.

"I actually got a packet like a week and a half ago from him with different pictures," laughed David Wright. "Erbe used to take baseball cards with like a position he thought was a good hitting position and photocopy it and send them to all of us. He would circle things and say, "this is what your elbow should look like" It was pretty amazing that he did it and did it for free. Nowadays, he probably could have made a killing with his instruction, and we were getting his time for free. The time and the effort he put in and still to follow up even through minor league, big league ball and now into retirement," said David Wright.

How did all the right coaches line up at the right time to make such a difference in David Wright's and the other players' lives and careers? The quick and easy answer may be that many coaches had players in the Blaster and Drillers organization. But the amount of skill, time, and leadership bought by Towny and his teammates was rare and free.

"We got kind of lucky to just kind of be in that age bracket, and no chance that happens now. I think about the amount of time they committed; it's amazing looking back on what the coaches gave up. It wasn't just traveling, the money spent on the weekends to go to these different tournaments, but also during the week we'd have practices, and during the summer, at times, we had two a day practices getting ready for big tournaments. Just the sacrifice for us, I don't think anybody would put that type of effort into and without compensation. I don't think it's a coincidence that in the same age group, it was myself and B.J. Upton. Just a little younger was Mark Reynolds and Josh Roupe. The list goes on and on. You can go even a little younger, and there is Chris Taylor. I think it's more luck who we got to coach us at such a young age and the leg up we all got as far as coaches go," said David Wright.

Ryan Zimmerman was one of the rabbits that Towny did not track down. Ryan Zimmerman is Mr. Driller and flourished and picked up much more than baseball from all the practices and tournaments he played in with the Drillers.

"We were obviously really good athletes and really good players, but they taught us how to be good people. But, at the end of the day, I was lucky I played baseball in the big leagues for 16 or 17 years, whatever it is," said Ryan Zimmerman.

The Blasters team helmed by Coach Alan Erbe certainly had some ups and downs, but they had fun as a team. The group began to age out to Legion and high school teams. Assistant Coach Ron Smith collected 60 short memories. Here are some of the best ones.

- How about the 20 pizzas and all the skin flicks the boys ordered in Cocoa Beach?
- How about the time we beat the Drillers by 10 runs when we were 12 after Coach Erbe strategically was tossed from the game for arguing a certain left-hander's (former Blaster, Kyle Breeden) pick-off move?
- How about the shot heard around the world? Dave Wright's gargantuan home run that knocked an oak branch off a tree in center field at the Junior Olympics—what a tape-measure shot!

- Who remembers Coach Erbe leaving Tennessee on his way to Wilmington, North Carolina, proclaiming he would look for some of the home run balls we gave up on his drive?
- Who could ever forget Brian Longboard's famous response to Coach Erbe the day we practiced at Alliance Christian in 100-degree-plus weather? Coach Erbe was pleading with the guys that it was going to be 20 degrees than this in Florida. Brian's response was, "Yeah, Coach Erbe, it is going to be 125 degrees in Florida." It seemed pretty funny at the time. I guess you had to be there.
- Hey Matt, what's the story of you skipping baseball practice to feed your girlfriend"s horses? Compliments of Dave W.
- How about the day David Wright hit 7 triples in a doubleheader against the Manassas Thunder in front of three Major League scouts when we were 12? We scored 52 runs in those 2 games, and I believe that was the day he had his first official Major League scouting card filled out. Heck, those guys wanted to sign the whole team!
- Three words: "naked at Shoney's" (if you don't get it, just ask some players).
- Is it true that Coach Erbe can navigate the country only using Waffle House maps?
- How about the time the coach from Durham protested our use of big-barrel bats, and then Dave Wright hit a home run with a first pitch using a Little League bat! Too bad we lost that game in the end.
- Didn't Dave Wright get sat down for throwing his helmet?

The endnote to the parents after the memories spanning from when the players were 12 years old to approximately 16 years old was from Coach Ron Smith and drove home what the team was about to the players and parents. In authentic Coach Townsend and Coach Erbe Blasters organizational philosophy, Smith's note was about the students, not the players.

> "I could probably come up with many more memories and even a few that aren't fit for print. Hopefully, this will raise a few memories for you and make some folks laugh. What's important is that we all started with some simple goals. We wanted to help these guys become the best baseball players that we possibly could. Our first goal was to prepare these boys for high school baseball. Every Blaster made their high school team as an eighth grader. We then focused on making them outstanding varsity players. Every Blaster was a varsity starter in 9th or 10th grade. We also focused on what it would take to make it to make the next level of college baseball. We didn't win a national championship, but more importantly, we remained true to ourselves and kept to our simple goals. We have more than a handful of guys that will play in college, and more importantly, most guys are successful students and are moving forward with college educations.
>
> "I think we succeeded! Parents, thank you for your support! Congratulations to all you guys and thanks for all the memories!"
>
> – Coach Smith

TEN:
NEVER TELL ME THE ODDS

The reality of professional sports is why coaches like Towny Townsend are so important. So many kids want to play professional baseball. Truth is that a minuscule number of players will ever be paid to put on a pair of cleats. Towny and the other coaches knew that and worked to enrich the person before the player. And even if they are ever paid to play a kid's game, it would still be such a small part of their relative life. Then what, were they going to be prepared as life moves on? Parents, mentors, and coaches stood ready for the Splendid 6 and all the players trying to reach the higher levels of the game.

Most fans just see and hear about players playing in the Major Leagues. The average Major League baseball career is approximately four years. Young men and women toil, work, and hope to stick on a

Minor League roster for a chance to hopefully get the call-up to the big leagues one day.

Many players do not have a reasonable chance and are kept around as organizational depth in the minor leagues with little to no opportunity to make the big-league club. It can be a cold and calculated business, with baseball not caring about the dreams and hopes of the player. Baseball is just a small amount of life the player probably played, trained, and sacrificed to do. Coaches like Matt Sinnen and Towny Townsend understood the harsh reality and wanted players to be ready for life, not just baseball.

Let's have a harsh look at the reality of wanting to make the Major Leagues as a youth. Approximately 15 million boys and girls a year play youth baseball. Only 10% of youth players climb through several ladders of rec ball, travel ball, to make a high school baseball team. Congratulations! That is a testament to keeping baseball fun, priority, hard work, dedication, and athletic ability!

Less than one high school player per 2,000 is drafted by a professional team. About five percent of players make a college team of any level of the NCAA. If you are one of those lucky ones, approximately 10% of those are drafted into the Minor leagues. And if you get to the Minor leagues, you are paid a barely livable wage. It ranges from $6,000 in Single-A to nearly $15,000 in Triple-A. Players are not paid in Spring Training or Fall Leagues. The poverty line of the United States is just below $13,000.

Players have worked on their craft for many years. At first, as a child playing a game. Then as a serious student of the game attempting to maintain a baseball scholarship or a spot on a professional roster. Most Major League players look to hit the milestones of reaching salary arbitration after three years, Free Agency after playing six years, and being fully tenured as a baseball player at 10 years to receive a full pension.

A player with 43 MLB days of service time qualifies for a maximum of $34,000 at 62 years of age old and can draw at a reduced rate at 45 years of age.

Only about 10% of players in the Minor Leagues will make an MLB Roster even for one day. However, Major League players of at least one day do get a lifetime Medical Plan. The percent of kids hitting bottlecaps or container lids that make Major League Baseball and have a career long enough to earn the full Major League pension is many zeroes below one percent. The number after several rounds of mathematics that the miniscule number spit out resulted in an almost melted calculator and blew my mind: 1.145e-22 or more precisely .00000000000000000001145%. The miracle of the Splendid 6 can only be partially quantified with a number including a letter. Each of the Splendid 6 had a 1.145e-22 percent chance of making it through all the many funnel points on and off the field to be able to hit 10 years MLB service time to qualify for the full pension. To have six players at the same general time from the area able to accomplish this is overwhelming and why they are the Splendid 6.

The average Major League career of three and three-fourths years does not pay millions per year or come with a comfortable medical and pension plan. Major League Baseball requires 10 years for the lifetime pension plan. Sixty percent of MLB players cannot even reach the salary arbitration milestone of three years. To put it into further perspective, the Society of Actuaries, in their 2018 stats, has approximately 22,250 people to be on a Major League roster in the history of Major League Baseball. There are just over 9,000 participants in the Major League Baseball Players Pension Plan. The average participant is at $53,000 annually.

The ever-changing MLB owners' unofficial business model of saving money and increasing profits is topping everything off. The MLB and their owners slashed away 43 Minor League baseball teams. As part of the reduced Minor League teams, the 2021 MLB Draft was cut in half from 40 to 20 Rounds. The MLB Draft was reduced in 2020—you know, COVID. The draft was reduced to 5 Rounds from the traditional 40 due to canceled sports, travel restrictions, and other considerations. The kicker was that no player could receive more than $100,000 on the bonus slot in 2020. The 2020 MLB first pick would usually be slotted to receive an $8,415,300 bonus and instead received a maximum of $100,000.

The 2021 Major League Baseball draft was 20 Rounds, down from the 40-round draft used for many years before that. As a result, the players drafted onto MLB teams were approximately 600, not the usual 1,200. The good news is that the 2022 Draft is back to 40 Rounds. But how long can potential baseball prospects count on the numbers not being lowered in the future? Especially with MLB looking to assimilate International Free Agents into a draft process.

The timeless classic movie "Dumb and Dumber" may have summed up the enthusiasm players, youth coaches, and parents have for the Major Leagues.

> ***Lloyd: Hit me with it! Just give it to me straight! I came a long way just to see you, Mary, Just... The least you can do is level with me. What are my chances?***
>
> ***Mary: Not good.***
>
> ***Lloyd: You mean, not good like one out of hundred?***
>
> ***Mary: I'd say more like one out of a million.***
>
> ***Lloyd: So, you're telling me there's a chance! YEAH!***

All baseball players have their last at-bat. For most, it may be in rec ball or high school, but the skilled and lucky ones take them in the Major Leagues like Ryan Zimmerman did in 2021.

"Eighty percent of my life is going to be spent not doing baseball. So, I thank them for teaching us how to be good people, respect other people, be a part of society, and be a part of our community. Those lessons are far more critical than teaching me how to hit a curveball or do anything on the baseball field. So, thank you for more than the baseball stuff, and honestly, when you're 12, 13 years old, I think teaching those lessons to that aged person can be a lot harder than teaching them how to play baseball," said Ryan Zimmerman.

Coaching a swing is one thing, but as players spend so much time with the coaches and players' parents, it is crucial to model the right behaviors and reinforce and understand baseball is a game. Most players have a tiny competitive window but can also contribute to learning fairness, equity, and competition. Unfortunately, lessons are not always easy to teach or learn.

"Those are the kind of tough lessons a lot of people don't want to teach people because it's hard. It is hard to be the voice of reason. It's hard to be the person who tells you not to be an idiot," said Ryan Zimmerman. However, the coaches, parents, and players were all part of the experience. "Thank you for teaching me those kinds of hard lessons as a young man, which is obviously carried over, and I will use them as a father and a husband. All of those are lessons; I'll use way more than I'll ever use baseball," said Ryan Zimmerman.

ELEVEN:

YOUTH BASEBALL, OR YOUTH PLAYING BASEBALL?

Travel baseball is now a massive industry in the United States. There are certainly advantages and disadvantages. However, some argue it may put too much pressure stress on the players, cause financial hardship, and line the pockets of opportunistic coaches or travel organizations.

"I think it's gone too far. It's supposed to be for the kids to play against better talent, advance their game, and have an opportunity to play at the next level. I don't have any first-hand account, but it's become a way for people to make money off the kids from the outside looking in. It seems like some coaches and organizations are trying to make money instead of what the Blasters were doing, trying to make better players, and then with Lee Banks his team to put those players on the field. So now if you can't pay, you can't play, and that is not fair to the kids," said Justin Upton.

Travel teams routinely are built and maintained on the reputation and talent of the coaches but kept through the results of the talent produced. Towny, Erbe, Wright, Sinnen, and others certainly had the reputation in the area as the best of baseball minds. But it was the eye to evaluate to see a player that could be made into a better player, intelligent kids with a high baseball IQ, and, importantly, a player that would not embarrass themselves, the travel organization, and their parents. Those requirements were put into contractual effect with each player and coach understanding the roles and responsibilities to each other. Once you became a Blaster under the nod of Towny, your place on the team was secure, not to be cut. No player was cut from the Blasters or paid a Travel Ball Organization fee. Those principles are practically unheard of in today's billion-dollar industry.

Coaches like Towny Townsend, Coach Allan Erbe, Coach Manny Upton, Coach Matt Sinnen, and Coach Gary Wright are perhaps anomalies in the industry, having never made a dime from their travel teams.

Travel baseball has changed tremendously since Towny started the Blasters in the 1990s. Travel sports as a whole is booming and has many different sports splitting and re-splitting the talent pool of athletes. If you can think of a sport, there is a travel team—baseball, basketball, soccer, lacrosse, wrestling, football, and golf. Teams fill out the landscape of fields across cities and towns each weekend and during the week for evening practices and games.

Manny Upton still keeps his hand in coaching. Each year he takes players to a tournament who otherwise wouldn't have the showcase experience. But the landscape is different now than he had with the Blasters and his players back in the day.

"The one thing all the guys had in common was they were hard workers, and they enjoyed being together. They wanted to practice, a desire to make it," said Manny Upton. "The kids now are Prima Donnas, individuals; they don't want to be a team. I still coach old school. Coaches don't handle the equipment. The players hit the balls, they go get them," Manny Upton said.

The travel baseball industry is approximately a $20-billion-a-year business. Places like Disney World bring in weekly youth baseball and softball tournaments. Disney's ESPN Wide World of Sports Complex promises to have the players walk in the footsteps of top athletes and play ball on the same fields. The jewel of the complex is the stadium that is available to the youth teams. Which kid would not want to play in the 9,500-seat stadium? A travel coach can feel like he is managing professionally. There are even four luxury skyboxes, multiple open-air suites, and patios to complete the fantasy scenario.

Every parent, coach, and kid's dream of playing and feeling like a professional can be had for the right dollar figure. If you don't want to play in a tournament, your youth travel baseball team can even have their "Spring Training" in Florida like Major League players for a team cost of approximately $1,300. Airfare, dining, and Walt Disney lodging are each sold separately per player, coach, and family.

Would Towny have fallen into the same traps? How did Hampton Roads baseball change over the years? Michael Cuddyer does not like the word "Travel"; he prefers the term "Club" to describe what today's teams should be and wonders what Towny could change today if he had the chance.

"Once Towny passed away, organization went away, and the area became the Wild West for travel baseball. I can only speak to this area, but now there are no rules: now it's make up a team, go play, steal a player, take this guy, whatever, I don't care if they are not a good player or a person, I'm taking them. I am not sure if Towny would have been able to stop it, but he would've been able to at least shape it," said Michael Cuddyer. "The showcase environment is so saturated now, but if you are good, the scouts will find you," explained Cuddyer.

Michael Cuddyer believes the coaches should teach the game, not so much as the specific parts of the game, but the general enthusiasm and love to play. The curiosity and fun in baseball are not what they once were, and neither are the players working on their own in the back yard, garage, or driveway. So instead, Michael Cuddyer helps to coach his 14-year-old son and his team. But for Michael Cuddyer, it is less about coaching and more about inspiring and instilling the youth.

"I enjoy trying to get the kids, like Towny did, to love something; to me, the content and instruction is secondary," explained Michael Cuddyer. "I don't think kids do dry swings by themselves in their garage anymore; that uncontrolled play goes a long way," said Michael Cuddyer.

Travel teams can be a harsh environment. Players come and go and float through teams as parents and players constantly look for the best opportunity for playing time, prestige of a team, blend of kids. Coaches can become egotistical, forgetting it is about the player and thinking of themselves and the need to take home a trophy first. Loyalty talked about and not practiced is rampant.

"I think my father would be sick from the travel ball system today," said Sean Townsend. "He intended it to be for kids that want to play harder and not just a glorified rec program, and he would be disappointed on how cost-prohibitive it has become," said Sean Townsend. "Not $150 a month-dues and all this stuff," Sean Townsend continued.

Each coach and organization should make a choice. Is it about winning for us, or is our goal to develop the best player and person we can be? The Blasters and Towny chose the latter. Make a better player and person. The Drillers also put money where their mouth is.

"Matt and I started a scholarship fund back when we first got the Drillers going. We raised about $30,000 a year through some golf tournaments to give back to the players in their first year in college. We are in the $200,000 range of scholarships earned over the years. Each year, for example, if we have $25,000 in the account and 25 people are applying, we will find a way to get $1,000 to each student. That's probably the biggest thing I'm proud of," said Gary Wright.

It is standard for travel ball organizations to recruit players from states away, even thousands of miles, with players just flying directly to the tournaments and rarely if ever practicing as a team. Not the Blasters; the players were not plucked from the hotbeds of traditional baseball talent—states like California, Florida, and Texas with warm year-round weather and baseball nonstop, and stocked with dominant players on the best travel teams with the pool of players committing to college baseball programs or ready to play Minor League baseball. The coaches looked to an area known for a murky large swamp. It could have been a dismal view.

TWELVE:
DISMAL SWAMP

The Hampton Roads is intertwined with a vast 112,000-acre area called the Great Dismal Swamp. Overlooked during history with a massive swath of beauty and natural resources, the name "Great Dismal Swamp" easily could be how Major League Baseball would have termed Hampton Roads.

The chances of finding prospects before Towny, his "Teammates," and like-minded individuals began to turn MLB's attention to the promising young men and baseball players of the region was slim.

You can't blame the scouts and colleges for overlooking the Hampton Roads area. It was simply not on the MLB radar. As a result, players drafted out of the area were few and far between. Towny was one of the few high-draft picks since the draft first began in 1965. Swoope, a few years later, was another.

Billy Swoope was a lifelong friend of Towny. "I first heard of and saw Towny back in Little League and as he played in high school at Lake Taylor High School Norfolk," explained Swoope. "Professional scouts heard of Towny and how good he played and began to put eyes on him. So, he gave players and me later on the hope the scouts would come around."

The professional scouts did come around after Towny signed for a short time and took Swoope out of Norfolk Catholic High School, making him their 10th-round pick of the 1976 Draft. Swoope began as a catcher and was blocked by the longtime Major Leaguer and future MLB manager, Mike Scioscia. A move to the outfield produced solid results for several years before retiring, reaching as high as Double-A and retiring from baseball in 1981. However, Swoope soon did what a couple of Towny's teammates would later do. Like Towny and Matt Sinnen, he coached at Virginia Wesleyan, even being named the NCAA's Division III Baseball Coach of the year in 1985. After that, Swoope shifted his focus and became the regional scout for the Chicago Cubs to include the Hampton Roads area.

"This area, Hampton Roads, was not a busy place in the 1980s and the early 1990s until the work of Towny and the others started to produce big-time prospects," said Swoope.

The players in the area being produced helped to make some solid draft plans for the Cubs based on the glowing reports being generated from the baseball swamp of Hampton Roads. Major League Baseball began to see all the talent and resources uncovered, refined, and displayed in Hampton Roads.

"The Chicago Cubs were going to pick Michael Cuddyer with the 10th pick of the 1997 MLB June Amateur Draft, but the Minnesota Twins selected him at 9th. I was heartbroken," said Swoope. In California, the Chicago Cubs took John Garland, a right-handed pitcher from Kennedy High School, Granada Hills. Garland was traded a year later after being drafted by the Cubs across town to the Chicago White Sox. Garland made an All-Star Team and an anchor of starting rotation of the 2005 World Series champion, the Chicago White Sox team. Cuddyer went on to win a Batting Title, Silver Slugger, and become a two-time All-Star. Eight of the first ten picks of 1997 were from hot weather states far away from the at times dismal weather of Hampton Roads.

History seemed to rear its ugly head again for Billy Swoope a few years later during the 2001 Draft, as two tremendous Hampton Road talents slipped past the Cubs. The Chicago Cubs had the second pick of the draft, selecting future All-Star pitcher Mark Prior, but had big plans for their second pick of the draft. "We had the second pick of the second round, and the Cubs were ready to pounce on David Wright with that pick, but the New York Mets beat us to the punch in the first round sandwich pick at 38," said Swoope. So instead, the Cubs took Andy Sisco, a left-handed pitcher who played in the Cubs farm system before being selected in the 2004 Rule 5 Draft and playing for the Kansas City Royal the same year. Sisco ended his Major League career in 2007 with Chicago across town. The White Sox.

Billy Swoope recommended the two local players, Cuddyer and Wright, to be drafted and signed by the Chicago Cubs, with both being narrowly missed. The two fish that got away were franchise players for the team drafting them. Michael Cuddyer was inducted into the Minnesota Twins Hall of Fame in 2017. David Wright's induction into the Met's Hall of Fame is a foregone conclusion after being perhaps the most popular player and successful position player in Mets history.

The most successful and popular player in Mets franchise history is Tom Seaver, the Ace of the amazing 1969 New York Mets World Championship team. Seaver had a Hall of Fame career and three Cy Young Awards as the National League's best pitcher. Seaver's Mets career lasted 10 years, 1967 to 1977, before being traded in 1977 in an unpopular move deemed the "Midnight Massacre." However, the great Met pitcher is so popular with fans that there is a road named after him, Seaver Way, near the baseball stadium, and a Tom Seaver statue was unveiled early in the 2022 season. David Wright will probably receive the same honors one day.

THIRTEEN:
ONE TIME AT BASEBALL CAMP

Before the Blasters and Drillers organizations started and helped so many players learn baseball, receive college academic or athletic scholarships, and perhaps even the chance to make a professional roster, Towny ran as many baseball camps as he could to help inspire baseball to the kids. The camps were the first opportunity for many players to receive their first intensive education at baseball. Towny and Gary Lavelle started running baseball clinics where and when they could. The costs of the camps were purposefully kept low to ensure kids were not left out. Towny and Lavelle were there to teach how to field the grounder and how to fall in love with the sounds and feel of being a player on the field.

Michael Cuddyer remembers going to any sports camp he could as a kid in Hampton Roads. If there was a ball in the 1980s and

1990s, Cuddyer was probably throwing or chasing it down on some floor or a grassy field.

Cuddyer played football, basketball, and baseball and took to the mat for wrestling. If those sports had a local clinic or a camp, Cuddyer and his parents would find it on weekends and during time off school. The Towny and Lavelle baseball clinics were about to hook a player so good that he would later earn a National League batting title.

"Towny did clinics because he loved kids and had a passion for baseball. I think that's what a youth coach's job is; it's not to get a kid a scholarship, it's not to teach him the greatest mechanics in the world," said Michael Cuddyer. "It is to put the fish-hook in the player, show them to love and have a passion for something," explained Cuddyer.

For kids, like Michael Cuddyer, looking up to Major League players, Gary Lavelle was a former player whose All-Star baseball card could be seen displayed in local card shops and maybe even in their own baseball collections, and Towny was a high draft pick by the Red Sox, a local high school playing legend drafted higher than any player in the area until Michael Cuddyer would be drafted. Towny and Lavelle, besides being a great name for a Motown band, were two men with an infectious love to teach and inspire the players, but also possessed the baseball skills to make the strongest of impressions on the baseball campers.

"I was an eight-year-old, and I just loved it. "I remember the first time I ever saw Coach Lavelle pitching; he wasn't too far from his playing days, and he was talking about location and being able to locate pitches," said Michael Cuddyer. "I just remember him throwing a bullpen and being able to hit every single target the catcher put up. I had never seen that before, somebody with that much control, that much accuracy," explained Michael Cuddyer.

Baseball camps can be big money nowadays with some kids not able to be part of it. But Towny would always find a way to be inclusive and encourage kids to be part of it, regardless of money or equipment. "Towny never knew a stranger. I got a call a couple years ago from a guy from our very first camp. He stayed at his grandfather's house across the street from Virginia Wesleyan and came over after seeing all the kids. He began just by hanging out at the fence," explained Cathy Townsend. "Towny walked over to him and asked him if he wanted to come in. The kid said he was staying with his grandparents and didn't have money. Towny said, come in; the kid then said he didn't have a glove. Towny then took off his glove, handed it to him, and told him to keep it. After all those years, the kid just called to let me know he still had that glove. That was my husband, Towny," said Cathy Townsend.

Towny Townsend and Gary Lavelle went weekend-to-weekend holding camps and teaching baseball. A young David Wright was another eight-year-old kid at one of those camps.

Even before David Wright became Mr. Blaster playing for Coach Erbe and Towny there was a sense of character, focus, and work ethic that could be built on. A Driller, not a Blaster, has one of the earliest tales of a young David Wright methodically working to become an "overnight" baseball prodigy and leaving a strong impression.

"The first time I saw David Wright, I was doing a camp, all the campers were being picked up, and you couldn't leave a camper alone," said Gary Wright, Co-Founder of the Drillers.

"A young kid was still hitting balls off the hitting tee in the batting cage. I went down there and asked 'how you doing, little fella.' David replied with 'Oh, hey coach.' I'll never forget it. He said, 'You know my last name is Wright too,' and I said 'No, what's your name?' He goes 'David, David Wright.'"

Young David explained his mom was at work and running late. But instead of being near the parking lot, he chose to be in the cages taking extra swings after all the camp work.

"I took a ball, put it on the tee, and I said, 'Let's see what you got.' There's this little kind of chubby kid about eight years old at that time. I said, 'holy smokes, Dave, where did you get that swing.' He goes 'I got I got it from my dad, he's a police officer.' He was talking to me like he was all grown-up. David's mom Elisa came walking up, and I said, 'you got yourself a pistol here' don't you?' and she said, 'yeah, and he will go home tonight after the camp, and he will go back outside for another hour and hit balls into a little blanket thrown over a clothesline, and then he will go to bed,' said Elisa Wright.

Young David Wright interrupted. "Coach, can I ask you a question?" David explained, "My daddy told me that if I outworked everybody, I might be a major leaguer someday." I said, "Well, probably can't hurt to go with that philosophy." "The kid was like eight years old, right? I was just sitting there thinking, wow, what a great kid," said Gary Wright.

David Wright throughout his career was known for his grit, work ethic, and baseball I.Q.

Even as a youngster those traits were being shaped and he didn't want to go to a baseball camp not able to help him be better or a waste of his family's hard-earned money and valuable time.

"My dad and my grandparents would send me to all kinds of sports camps during summers. As I got older, I realized which camps were a waste of time and better. The camps by Towny Townsend and Gary Lavelle had reputation and street cred because of their professional baseball experience," David Wright explained. "They had great instruction and good kids that knew how to play the game, and I fit in. Some camps were more like babysitting with kids running around and goofing off for a couple of hours," continued David Wright. "Towny's camps were different. Towny and Gary (Lavelle) would put us in the bleachers and make us answer trivia questions or teach us about the game and about different players. We even memorized the poem 'Casey at the Bat.' Towny would teach life lessons through baseball, and it always stuck with me," explained David Wright. "I like intensity and focus. I didn't want to be babysat. I wanted to work to get better, and his camps were the perfect place for it," said David Wright.

Towny and Gary Lavelle's baseball camps occasionally were able to have baseball camps with nearby Old Dominion University, which invited older and accomplished retired and active professional ballplayers as instructors. Imagine being a kid and Bob Gibson is helping you with your fastball or Will Clark and Johnny Bench talking about hitting? Towny, Gary Lavelle, and ODU baseball connections made those camps possible with no cost to the players. These accomplished players, some of them Hall-of-Famers, would appear for free. The expenses for the camp were sponsored by local companies eager to help the community and attach their names to some baseball legends.

Michael Cuddyer still has an instructor sheet autographed by all the coaches. One name is highlighted and prominently displayed in a frame in his baseball office: Hank Aaron. Access to the man who had to play through racial static and still be able to pass Babe Ruth's career HR record of 714 and extend it to 755 was what Towny and his friends could bring to the local players. Many baseball fans still consider Hank Aaron as the record holder even though Barry Bonds hit 762.

"It was cool when there was an ODU Baseball Camp. We would run into all these old players, and they would teach you how to model yourself if you ever made it to professional baseball. After I was drafted by the Mets, I came out and helped run one," said David Wright.

Signing a professional contract as a teenager with your favorite team is, for most, a dream true but can often lead to some disappointment. "Don't meet your Heroes, you may be disappointed" is not something David Wright perpetuated as he wore the Met's uniform at baseball clinics and even played for the Triple-A team in Norfolk.

"I used to go the camp, and then years later I am in a Mets uniform, and the kids are asking me for pictures. So, it was like a full circle sort of thing. It's like that when I played for the Tidewater Tides, I remember going down toward the field at Norfolk Tides games to try to get autographs as a kid," said David Wright. "The scout that drafted me was Randy Milligan. So, I remember going to Norfolk Tides games at the Old Met Park and screaming at him with my mom and dad, and then suddenly, he's showing up at my door talking to me about the minor leagues in the Mets and maybe being drafted by the Mets," said David Wright.

SEAVER
SEAVER
1967-1977, 1983

citi FIELD
Nikon
Mets

1996 AAU NATIONAL
CHAMPIONSHIPS
12 & UNDER
VIRGINIA BLASTERS
BVILLE-LKVILLE, MN

BLASTERS

USA
BASEBALL
2001 USA BASEBALL
CHAMPIONSHIPS-EAST
JUPITER, FLORIDA

FOURTEEN:
THROUGH PARENTS' EYES

David Wright's mother and father, Elisa and Rhon, were a good old-fashioned high school romance. After they were married, they worked separately at auto dealerships and then the local Navy Exchange. Elisa became a Teacher's Assistant and then a School Security Officer. Rhon's path took him to the Norfolk Police Department, where duties and roles included K-9 Unit, Swat Team, and even undercover for the vice and narcotics division before becoming Norfolk's assistant chief of police. David and his three younger brothers, Stephen, Matthew, and Daniel, were not going to get away with much. Their mentors and spheres of influence would be carefully selected, just like Towny picked the kind of parents and players he wanted.

"We first met Towny with David in 1993; David was 9 or 10. They had just opened an indoor batting cage called Grand Slam; up until then, David was a sort of a seasonal athlete. He would play basketball during basketball season, football during football season, and baseball during baseball season. This was really the first opportunity because of the temperature, shorter days, and inclement weather to do some additional baseball training. Baseball seemed to be David's favorite sport, so we would bring David there. They had a neat pro shop, a birthday party room, and all the typical stuff. We went enough to see the same faces. We became acquainted with the owners and the employees that worked there. That's how we began to first notice and learn of and see Towny," explained Rhon Wright.

As Rhon Wright noticed Towny Townsend, it seems Towny Townsend noticed as well.

"Townsend was giving private lessons there, but David never took any instructions from him, most probably because we couldn't afford it at the time, but it was nice being around him. Towny would offer words of encouragement to the kids hitting in the cage, and towards the Summer, he offered me a pamphlet for a baseball camp he ran in the summer. With Towny's credentials, having coached at the collegiate level, a high school coach, and he also played professional baseball, we decided to let David go," said Rhon Wright.

Towny could quickly see what players possessed the mindset, skills, and desire to learn and used his baseball clinics to identify those players.

"David went to that camp, and he did fairly well. I didn't go as I was working shiftwork at the time. My dad took David to the week-long camp. On the last day of the camp, my dad called me and said Coach Townsend wanted me to call him. During the call, Towny went over what a coach would do at the end of any camp. What needed to be worked on and what seemed to be strengths. He then said he was looking to put together a baseball team for a tournament and if David wanted to play. So, we went to the weekend tournament in Vienna, Virginia," said Rhon Wright.

The team was primarily based on the Great Bridge, Chesapeake, Virginia area. Towny put together two teams from the area, an A team and a B team, a red team, and a white team.

"There was no promise of playing time as David was one of the younger players on the team, but he would get some playing time. Of course, I am a biased parent, but David did fairly well. He hit a home run," explained Rhon Wright. "After that tournament, and it may have been in the works all along, Towny decided that he and some coaches would start the Blasters organization," explained Rhon Wright.

The Blasters were Chesapeake-based 10 and under, 11 and under, 12 and under, as AAU teams. David at first started to play within the organization a year ahead, holding his own, but perhaps his own age group would be the best for the player. "Down the line, they decided to place David in his proper age group. That is how we met Coach Allan Erbe," said Rhon Wright.

"If not for Towny, the way he handled and conducted himself, his baseball knowledge and of course he was very articulate, smart as a tack with a high IQ, everything working together, I am not sure any of it would have ever happened," said Rhon Wright, David Wright's father.

Towny was the glue, inspiration, and organizer for the Blasters teams. He started it all, oversaw the various age levels, and made the final call on the organization's direction, but each team had its respective coaches. The players were from anywhere they could find the right kind of kid for the Blasters and the team. Towny Townsend used the same principles of development with his high school coaching.

"The goal was to develop the kids, to bring out the best in them and teach life lessons through baseball. Towny was the Head Coach at Lake Taylor High School in Norfolk. Baseball was not a real popular sport. Football and basketball were, but he would get those kids to come out and work with them and routinely win district titles. Towny could see a kid's strengths and weaknesses and build on them and, in general, just help the kid. If the kid was good at baseball, it was a plus, but generally, he just focused on making a better person," said Rhon Wright.

Youth and travel sports of any kind can help keep kids out of trouble and enable parents to actively see and interact within the spheres of a child's influence. For the Wright family, that was important, and the organization and coaches had to be the right fit for them.

"The Blasters were an opportunity I thought as a father, as a parent, to sort of steer your child in the right direction. I'm a retired police officer, and one of the things I noticed early on in my career was idle kids had a propensity to get in trouble," said Rhon Wright. "I didn't really care as a parent what our children did as long as they were doing something. It could be the Chess Club or ROTC. It didn't matter. I wanted him to be doing something, and the Blasters were a great option," explained Rhon Wright.

"You must give that credit to Towny and Allan Erbe. I think it was sort of instilled in the Blasters organization. Let's make the kids baseball savvy and hit the ball 400 feet. I think they were marching in unison for the players," said Rhon Wright.

Towny would show up at games and tournaments with the other age groups even when he was not coaching, to check and see how things were going.

"The coaches talked on the phone, and Towny was very much the Admiral of the Fleet. He was the one calling the shots. I think he was a good influence over the whole organization. We felt fortunate and blessed to have the honor of Towny being our coach and being with his coaches," said Rhon Wright.

The players had to be smart too, not just baseball savvy. The goal from the beginning was for each kid to be a starter on their high school baseball teams and be in line for college scholarships. Players had to sign a contract agreeing to a 2.5 GPA. But for many of them, it was not a problem. David Wright had a 4.0-plus weighted GPA, Michael Cuddyer a 4.0-plus weighted GPA, and Ryan Zimmerman and Mark Reynolds earned scholarships to the highly academically selective University of Virginia.

The Blasters were about excellence on the field, looking good while doing it, and behaving right on and off the field.

"I was huge on education, and I'm sure Towny was too. It wasn't just grades; it was other things too. Know how you look, don't have your shirttail hanging out, don't throw your helmet when you strike out. I know one of the things that kids always had to do was polish their cleats before every game," said Rhon Wright. "I like the discipline because being a police officer as a paramilitary organization, I spent time in the Army and Reserves in the National Guard, I was sort of a strict parent and liked the discipline," explained Rhon Wright.

The Blasters concentrated not just on a first and third play or taking the ball the other way; details can change outcomes no matter how small or seemingly insignificant. The Blasters were taught that the details matter.

"If you take care of the little things, like polishing your cleats before every game even though they're going to look terrible by the end of the day, it teaches the player to do something before going on the field. It was those kinds of tasks that instilled responsibility in those kids at an early age and helped them as a team, but also as they advanced into adulthood," said Rhon Wright.

Rhon Wright tried to be David Wright's baseball coach. Like many parents, they started out in the living room, backyard, driveway, basically anywhere a ball could be thrown. David's mother, Elisa, would often be out there as well. Teaching the love of baseball is usually from home first. But once David joined a team, it became more complicated.

"I coached him in Little League. David will probably tell you that I was a horrendous coach, that I put him in the outfield when he should have been a middle infielder somewhere. I've heard the story 10,000 times from him. Part of it was developing David and demonstrating you're not entitled to anything because your dad's a coach. You must earn playing time and your position. You must show not only me, but also the skeptical other parents that you deserved an at-bat or some spot in the batting order. It was another opportunity to instill life lessons into David. I like baseball too, so it was fun out to be out there competing and trying to out-manage the other manager," said Rhon Wright.

Rhon eventually and smartly put his kid at the most prestigious spot, usually holding the best athlete and player on a youth team, shortstop. Having a kid at shortstop handling the left side of the field that would eventually become a Major League Gold Glover should have been an easy and quick decision; but David had to earn shortstop first and held it all the way until the Mets made him a third baseman.

"When I made a move and put him at shortstop, there was no issue with the parents. I don't know if it was because they appreciated David's skill level at the time, or it was some sort of inherent respect for the coach. Or if it was, I was a cop, and maybe they were worried I was going to pull him over and give them a ticket," said Rhon Wright. "Of course, I never would have done that," he said.

Lineup decisions of coaches are always second-guessed. Rhon Wright was no different as he coached David's youth team. But he tried to be prepared for it.

"I didn't know why they would complain sometimes, and it drove me absolutely nuts at times. At playing time, it was like, you know why "Johnny" is playing over "Billy," said Rhon Wright. "I really enjoy stats. I would do my best to keep stats, and I tried to make it so that if somebody came up and complained about their child's playing time, I could pull out stats and say he's batting a buck and a quarter," explained Rhon Wright.

Some of the kids were being developed into the players scouts navigated to the ends of Virginia to see. But even the parents of the Splendid 6 never suspected nor saw it as a path being paved to the Major Leagues, and possibly one day millions of dollars in contracts with the admiration of millions of fans in their future Major League stars.

The Lee Banks showcase team had the best Drillers and Blasters close to the same ages: David Wright, Ryan Zimmerman, B.J. Upton, Mark Reynolds, and the proverbial little brother hanging around in Justin Upton. The team was called the Tidewater Mets.

"Most of the years David played, his teams were sponsored by somebody from the Mets organization. So, I always thought that was kind of cool," said Rhon Wright.

The team was not formed like many other teams at the time. Instead, it was just a small regional team, a Chesapeake and Virginia Beach team. The expectations were not that high or did people think that the core of the team would be perhaps the greatest local concentration of baseball talent in history.

"I don't remember anybody saying they were going to be three, four, or five All-Stars someday. I got the impression we realized we had a good team, though. You only know what's in your sphere of knowledge. You don't know what's going on in Omaha, Nebraska. They were all kids, doing good," explained Rhon Wright.

As the players went against the more seemingly established players from different areas, the Tidewater Baseball Boys were more than competing; they excelled as a team and stood out as individual players. But were they pro potential?

"When you talk to David, he will say he knew he was pro material from about the third grade," laughed Rhon Wright. "I was not even thinking of that. It was just more of a case of how David is doing, more than really paying attention to anybody else. I never compared him at all to anybody. I think it was as much a defense mechanism for me because I didn't want to get my hopes up that he's going to do this or do that," explained Rhon Wright. "It was always, let's go and do good in school, play high school ball, let's, graduate. Go to college and then start working 40 hours a week at whatever your chosen profession turns out to be," said Rhon Wright.

The idea of their child being drafted by a Major League baseball team and signing a professional contract bypassing college is intense pressure. For Rhon and Elisa Wright, it was no different.

"I never said he was going to be a professional baseball player, even to David. People would come up and say, "Hey, he's pretty good," or when he started getting interest from colleges and universities and even after Major League scouts started coming around," said Rhon Wright,

"David committed to Georgia Tech and signed his national letter of intent. Even after he got drafted, we were still buying shower caddies with the Georgia Tech logo on them. We just didn't want to tell ourselves he's going to be a pro player, and we're not going to worry about him making money or to forget about college," said Rhon Wright.

According to Rhon Wright, the management of expectations and being grounded were essential tools for David and the family during the process.

"It almost came to the last second that we believed he would become a professional baseball player. It was more for us than him, but I think it kept him humble in large part. The "Wait a second, you have not signed any contract yet?" and "You haven't proven anything on the field yet," or "You haven't passed your first semester down in Atlanta"—it was that "You have not done anything" attitude that helped, explained Rhon Wright.

David Wright made his decision to sign his professional contract with the Mets. The agreement also included a provision for up to $15,000 for eight semesters. David did not use his college plan, but it was a benefit and an additional consideration to make bypassing college easier for David and his parents. Major League Baseball's college plan is administered with the signing team responsible for the expenses. The scholarship is good for the length of the playing career and two additional years after the last day of professional service.

Many parents value a college education as a way for their children to acquire the tools for the best job career and to provide financially. Although David Wright retired as a player and appears to be financially set, his college education is still a goal they want for David.

"Even though the plan has now expired, Elisa and I still hope he will go back to school someday," said Rhon Wright.

FIFTEEN:
TIDEWATER LOYALTY

The Blasters avoided some of the pitfalls and temptations in youth sports. However, loyalty meant something and had to be shared.

"The other parents and the kids were great. The Blasters never cut anybody because they weren't good enough. The Blasters had loyalty. It was two-way, though: show me loyalty, and we return the favor. The kids got along great, and we never had any problems," said Rhon Wright.

Loyalty is such an important lesson to learn in life. It is often discussed but not modeled as often as it needs to be. The sense of loyalty and team was pounded into the players by parents and coaches alike. Parents, players, and coaches would often live by their team's choices. If a player had a bad game, tournament, losing playing time, or preferred position, it would be easy to look at what another organization offers. If a player goes 0-4 with four strikeouts and a couple errors in the field, the coaches may be tempted to look for another player. Not with the Blasters; players were more than cogs in the wheel to make a coach look good or a parent to walk around with their chest all puffed up. It was a long-range vision and journey the player, coaches, and parents agreed to take together.

In today's era of free agency and salary implications for Major League teams, it is almost unheard of for a player to be drafted, play through the Minor Leagues, and then further play 10 or more years for the Major League franchise.

Both David Wright and Ryan Zimmerman played their entire Major League careers with one franchise. Michael Cuddyer was also drafted by the Minnesota Twins, played through their farm system, and then 10 more years on their Major League club.

"It was bred early on, a sense of loyalty for the team. I think it's so hard to do that at the big-league level now at any professional sports level because economics and business are involved. People don't understand how hard it is for both sides to want to do it. So, we went through kind of that mutual respect and saw how, somewhere at the beginning, how building a legacy is awesome and fun to do," explained Ryan Zimmerman of the Washington Nationals.

"When I got to the Major League level, I would say it felt natural. I think David Wright and I were lucky to land in the situations we landed in. It takes a lot of things to happen right to even have the ability to be in that situation like we landed into," said Zimmerman. "We both got there relatively young and had success quickly in our careers. Even at a young age, with the Blasters and Drillers, we had that sense of loyalty from and to those teams, and we both have really good parents.

"I met David's parents a couple times and talked with David, a bunch about his mom and dad, his family, and growing up. They taught David to do the right things and be a good person. David's parents are a lot like mine," said Zimmerman. "I think we can give credit to the Drillers and Blasters. I also think we were both fortunate to have an awesome family structure where loyalty and following through on what is said and doing things the right way was built in us even way before baseball started for us," said Zimmerman.

Travel baseball parents and players tend to bond as they go away to play in tournaments, or when practices force parents to divide duties such as driving to and from the events. Long days at the fields are followed by impromptu team lunches and dinners. A pool party will break out as more kids and parents find the hotel pool. A cocktail hour may develop in the lobby for parents as players go to bed. It can take a parent and coach village to care for a team, and the memories last a lifetime.

The Drillers under Coach Matt Sinnen and Coach Gary Wright projected many of the same values for players like Ryan Zimmerman.

"We were lucky as kids to have a collection of parents and families that we're such good influences on all of us to the point if my family or my mom and dad couldn't make a weekend trip, I could go with another player's parents on our Driller team. So, we knew 100% it was going to be fine. It was almost like we were raised by a bunch of different parents that all had the same values," said Ryan Zimmerman.

An old 1996 Chevy Suburban still graces David Wright's parent's Chesapeake driveway. The odometer reads over 260,000 miles.

At least 200,000 of those miles hold the cherished memories of early morning and late-night drives on the roads and highways to Orlando or Cocoa Beach in Florida and whatever tournaments or practices the Wrights shuttled their kids to.

"I can remember just me and David driving for hours. I think that was good parent–child time together; we wouldn't have had it at all if not for baseball. Even as a family going on vacation, you don't get the time together talking like that," explained Rhon Wright.

The cost of time and money for baseball and time off work can be a considerable challenge for some parents, but there was peace of mind knowing they were around like-minded individuals and players.

"We did a lot back and forth driving and spent a lot of money. But, I think we thought it was worth it because you can't put a value on keeping your kid out of trouble or helping to develop their social relationships with friends," said Rhon Wright.

Even the occasional indiscretion was reasonably benign for the parents and players. For example, teams often go out for a meal after a long day at the field with one of the parents organizing. Naturally, the question to the kids was where they wanted to go for food and this time the mischievous side of 10-year-olds came through as they proposed the choice to an unsuspecting mom.

"After a big win, one of the moms brought the kids to Hooters. They were 10-years old or something. I thought it was pretty funny. I'm not sure Towny knew of it or approved," laughed Rhon Wright. "I can honestly say all the kids and their parents we met over the years from t-ball right up to even now, I don't think I ever met one bad baseball person that wanted to try to lead his or her teammates astray," said Rhon Wright. "I think it was money well spent.

We weren't rich, we were both working, but we just tried to put our money towards stuff we did, like car washes and donut sales to help save and raise money," explained Rhon Wright.

Those player and parent connections followed through for the two players who were not drafted in their respective MLB Drafts but went off to play in college. Ryan Zimmerman and Mark Reynolds were on some of the same showcase teams and part of the Driller's organization. Their baseball paths intertwined once again when Zimmerman went to the University of Virginia and played next to Mark Reynolds.

"Mark was a year ahead of me, and he was a Freshman All-American. I signed to go to Virginia; I only played shortstop; I'd never played third base before in my life. I got there in the Fall, and the coaches said Mark was a Freshman All-American last year, and we're not moving him from shortstop," said Zimmerman. They then asked Zimmerman if he had ever played third base. "I said no, and they said, well if you want to play, you're going to have to play third base. I said, Well I guess I'm playing third base," laughed Zimmerman. "Mark and I became pretty close that year. We knew each other in high school, but we became closer in college," explained Zimmerman.

Those reestablished bonds and connections were strong between players and parents as well.

"Sometimes we would just grab Ryan at the field and take him with us, to lunch, dinner wherever we were going; we called him our adopted son," said Tammy Reynolds, mother to Mark Reynolds.

Zimmerman was a freshman, didn't have a car, and lived on campus. Reynolds, a sophomore, lived off-campus and had a car.

"When Winter Break and Fall Break and things like that would happen, we could go home. I didn't have a car my freshman year, so

Mark would drive me home and take me back," said Zimmerman. "It was just kind of that thing where you take care of people and because we knew each other and because we were from the same area," explained Zimmerman.

Loyalty and mutual respect ran deep with the baseball players from the 757 area code. "We were kind of bred to take care of people from the Tidewater area. We're all baseball players from this area. It's kind of like a club that you're in, and you take care of each other," explained Zimmerman. If Reynolds's parents came up, they would take Zimmerman out as well.

"They would always invite me to all their stuff. I can remember so many dinners in college they took me to. When you get to go out for a nice dinner in college, it's a huge deal; every time they came into town, they were doing stuff to help me out," said Zimmerman. "They definitely helped to take care of me a ton at Virginia," explained Zimmerman.

SIXTEEN: A PATH NOT TAKEN

Several players on those teams went on to hear the cheers from thousands of fans in a Major League stadium and millions more from TV screens at home each night. Even an occasional boo was also heard, but of course, no player wants to admit to hearing the boos.

One of those players would never hear those. The player, who some say, was a hitter as good as any of them, and with perhaps even more power and an excellent pitcher: Vincent Sibal.

"I would say Vince had the most power of the kids when they were young," said Rhon Wright. Coach Erbe, who coached Vince Sibal, describes him as a dominant player with great power as a lefty pitcher and a batter. Coach Erbe remembers Vince Sibal as an excellent player, but he always felt his heart may not have been it. "He was not as competitive as the other kids. I think he was playing because his parents wanted him to," said Coach Erbe.

Coach Allan Erbe kept excellent statistics for the 1995 12U AAU Blasters team. David Wright hit .555 with 8 home runs, 24 doubles, 15 triples, and 116 RBI in 218 at-bats. Vince Sibal batted .347 with 8 home runs, 13 doubles, 5 triples, and 78 RBI in 173 at-bats. Vince Sibal also went 10-2 with a sizzling 1.48 ERA and 80 Ks in 66.1 innings pitched. Vincent Sibal was also an excellent fielder, as his .971 fielding percentage led the team (min. 100 ABs played). Vince Sibal had 6 errors as a first baseman/outfielder and pitcher for the season. David Wright put up an outstanding .961 fielding percentage as shortstop.

The 8 home runs by Wright and Sibal in 1995 may seem relatively low, but many of the games were played with high school baseball field dimensions. It would not be outlandish to think many of the doubles and triples would have cleared the traditional 12 U fences. It potentially could have been 47 home runs in only 218 at-bats (an HR every 4.6 AB). For Vince Sibal, it could have been 26 home runs in 173 at-bats (an HR every 6.6 AB).

Before David Wright was jacking home runs during the Major League All-Star Home Run Derby with Michael Cuddyer, he was stroking home runs with Vince Sibal at a Home Run Derby as well. The 1995 AAU National Championship tournament in Burnsville, Minnesota, featured David Wright and Vince Sibal teaming up during the 1995 12U AAU National Championship Home Run Derby.

Vincent Sibal later played varsity baseball at Salem High School and shifted his attention and focus away from baseball afterward.

Vince Sibal is good with his baseball path not explored or taken. David Wright took a path away from Georgia Tech and turned to professional baseball and the adulation of millions of fans. Vince Sibal turned to James Madison University and Virginia Tech, graduating, and having a stellar and continued career with Microsoft.

In 2006, the year David was making his first All-Star team, Vince was about to graduate from Virginia Tech. That spring Vince reached out via David Wright's MLB Blog to encourage and further show his support for his former teammate. Vince himself was about to embark to the Left Coast to begin a career with Microsoft in Seattle. The note:

> Hey Dave,
>
> Glad to see you're doing so well. Nice hit the other day against the Braves. This is Vince Sibal from back home. It's been a really long time, and hopefully, I'll get to come to see you play soon. I recently found out your brother is here at Virginia Tech. I'm graduating from Tech this May and moving to Seattle to work at Microsoft. I'm trying to see you play before I leave, though, possibly in May against Phil. Anyway, hope you continue with the success.
>
> – Vince

David Wright, of course, got back to Vince Sabal. Unfortunately, the timing didn't work out for Vince and baseball schedules to meet with David. But according to Vince, they still kept in touch for some time after. Although Vincent Sibal is happy with his life, there are still times he wishes he pushed himself harder and perhaps tried to play after high school.

"I wish at least I played college baseball. I wish I didn't actively tell my parents I didn't want to play baseball anymore. I told my coach I didn't want to do it anymore. I think I didn't have the right mentors. If I lived a house down from David Wright, I would have wanted to compete as much as him in high school. My dad would tell me, "David's practicing in the morning each and every day." "I told him that "I didn't care." I do wish I had the right circle of friends around me at the time; maybe I would have done what I should of.

Vince Sibal is not sure if his father mentioned during middle school the possibility of moving to another school district first to him, or if he first mentioned it. The potential move of school districts would have been to an area where Vince could be at a more competitive high school baseball program like Great Bridge or Hickory.

"I remember David lived in a neighborhood close to mine, and then he moved to Chesapeake, it became a good move for him," explained Sibal. The Sibal family did not move toward Chesapeake. And instead, Vince went to Salem High School and played varsity baseball there. "Later, it really showed a difference. If you look at Hickory and Great Bridge, there was a lot of talent that came through," said Sibal. "A lot had to do with the coaching. I remember playing against those teams in high school, and I could tell their coach was very advanced. I think it was shortsighted my parents didn't see moving as valuable, looking back at the data, I would have been better off and probably more excited to compete. I just kind of burned out in high school," explained Sibal.

Vince Sibal wanted badly to do well, but it always felt it would not be good enough at home. My mother had an "it's never enough sort of strategy; she didn't have the experience to know what I needed to be and what to work on. I could never be or do enough with baseball for her. It just became exhausting for me," explained Sibal.

Coaching styles are a hard find for youth baseball players. Not every player responds the same way, and Vince Sibal was no exception. However, Vince Sibal wanted approval and support, and he did get that from Coach Erbe.

"Coach Erbe was supportive of me and not critical. He was a good coach for me mentally. I was always seeking his approval. I knew he would believe in us as players and teach us the right things. He constantly reinforced we were always getting better with the right touch of never enough. His coaching style was right for us," said Sibal.

For moments in Vince Sibal's baseball life, he believed he was as good or at times or even better than some of the players of the Splendid 6 who would later go on to the Major Leagues and the adulation of millions of fans.

"At the time, especially middle school and coming into high school, I saw myself as a very good and gifted baseball player. I saw them as competitors and peers, and they were fun to play with," said Vince Sibal of players in the Splendid 6.

"We had no clue of the potential that existed. But I did get a chance to experience that level like only a select few people would ever understand," said Vince Sibal, with a voice that even all the years later filled with pride and a touch of perhaps of a little something lost.

It seems like a young David Wright respected Vince Sibal and wanted to form a Batman and Robin, a 1-2 punch relationship. A little chubby but ultra-talented David Wright could see the skills in, at the time, a bigger and perhaps stronger player who was the lefty pitcher and power-hitting Vince Sibal. For years, Vince Sibal often batted fourth with David Wright protecting him in the lineup and batting fifth.

"David actually recruited me to the Blasters. We knew each other from Little League, playing and competing against each other in games and contests. Our teams would be in the Finals every time against each other. "I always wanted to be the best, I'm sure he felt the same way, keep in mind we were 12-year-olds, and he was different then, not yet the special baseball player we all saw with the Mets," said Vince Sibal.

Baseball was baseball to Wright and Sibal. If the Blasters weren't playing, they would seek each other out to help round out other teams to get more games in.

"David and I were friends, and baseball really is a small community. Other teams would sometimes need players to come in to help during a tournament. David and I would be the only two Blasters there, together, helping out for a week with the team," explained Vince Sibal.

Good players wanted to get better and compete against players sharing similar mindsets and goals. Vince Sibal was about to go from the basic coaching of Little League and a simplified playing construct into the mind and practices of Coach Allan Erbe and his lab and advanced school of baseball.

"Coach Erbe was one of the most unique teachers I ever had. I went from the 10's in Little League to the 11 through 13 teams under Coach Erbe. It went from being planted on each base to leading off the base, learning how to bunt and steal," said Vince Sibal.

The practices with Coach Erbe were different than anything Vince Sibal saw before or since and allowed Vince Sibal to compete against players that would be making the Major Leagues.

"Coach Erbe was really advanced in teaching us different tricks and techniques and ways to help me as a pitcher. We had great practices where we were just practicing first and third drills and ways to score from there. He was really unique in how he taught us. Coach

Erbe was big on inside-out hitting and taking it the other way. For a few of us, unlocking that skill helped us develop our power," said Vince Sibal.

By Vince Sibal's own admission, maybe he peaked with physical maturity too early and went from being the biggest and strongest kid on the team to falling behind as they went through high school.

Vince Sibal topped off as a rather large, for leaving middle-school, five-foot-ten-inch and 170-pound frame. After the four years of high school and into college when males usually boost and grow remarkably, Vince was still only five-ten and maybe a 180-pounder playing as a senior in high school. Vince is not sure that even with the best coaching and mentor network in place, he could have advanced up the past the high school baseball level and into college or professional baseball, but maybe he would have liked to have tried if the situation was a little different at the time. Vince played high school baseball and well by most standards, even making several of the area's Baseball Post Season Recognition teams.

The years for Vince Sibal after the AAU Virginia Blasters with the baseball coaching and mentorship of Towny Townsend and Allan Erbe left a gap for Vince Sibal playing in high school. Vince Sibal didn't feel the attention and level of coaching were the same, and he fell behind.

"I do wish I could have had more mentors like Allan Erbe in high school. After my 13's and going into high school, the coaching was a little behind. I just didn't have the same kind of mentorship as the other players. Some of them transferred into schools like Hickory and others into private schools. So, it was more difficult for me when I was on the Lee Banks Showcase team," said Vince Sibal.

Vince Sibal was thrown back into a deep talent pool of players like David Wright, Ryan Zimmerman, B.J. Upton, Justin Upton, and Mark Reynolds. Vince Sibal, in size, strength, and ability, did not progress during high school like the other players did and he could not stand out like when he was a Blaster with Coach Erbe. The Major League scouts and college coaches were not noticing Vince Sibal.

"The scouts were scouting David and B.J., and the players we all know now, as well as some of the other guys. I did not have a good scouting report at the time," said Sibal. "I was four years removed from last playing with the Blasters, it was just night and day in terms of what I messed up on," explained Sibal.

Even years later, Vince Sibal still has respect and loyalty to his former coaches. Vince Sibal paused for a second to regroup himself and to ensure his high school coaches would not take offense. "Please don't think it is anything against my coaches in high school; I just didn't have coaches with the same experiences or skills as they did," said Sibal.

SEVENTEEN:
THE SHOWCASE

Vince Sibal was still good enough to be on the Lee Banks Showcase team with stud players like Wright, Zimmerman, Reynolds, and the Uptons.

"Playing on that team felt normal to me, and first, I saw them as teammates and peers. I didn't watch those players and ever think they were going to become Major League All-Stars, because I was one of them," explained Sibal. "What I did see was how much more they matured physically, kept learning, and how much better they became. I knew they had passed me up, and it felt like a real difference as compared to me," said Sibal.

David Wright remembers playing on the Lee Banks showcase team in many ways, helping to cement him as a player and a baseball prospect.

"It is pretty cool looking back on the Coach Lee Banks Showcase team. It was weird because we all wanted to play shortstop. We were natural shortstops at our high school. Coach Banks mixed it up, and I played a little third and B.J. played some short. We all just moved around. Looking back on it now, it was a pivotal moment, obviously a little later in the game, the culture became multiple positions. But another pivotal moment was getting a chance to practice with these guys and play with them on the weekends. "You're pushing yourself, without even knowing it, you're competing against future All-Stars," explained David Wright.

Sometimes good players can be made great by the level of competition around them. The constant internal push to play well and stand out even among the best. David Wright used the players' competition around him to fuel him even further, propelling him into his senior year of high school and baseball.

"You think it's just a casual Wednesday practice at First Colonial High School. But in reality, everybody wants to be, in a still-friendly competition, the alpha of the team. Everybody wants to be the reason why the scouts are coming to watch this team," said David Wright.

"Although we were best of friends, we always wanted to be the guy, the reason people were coming out to watch. That's not bad, and it was as good as it gets as far as pushing yourself every practice, every game competing, against guys that would go on to be later competing for Major League All-Star Games and having incredible Major League careers. We were in high school competing, pushing each other, and becoming better and better. It was a great situation for all of us," explained David Wright.

Justin Upton is only perceived as the "Bat Boy" of the team, but he played some off the bench, a huge accomplishment for a player almost five years younger than David Wright and some of the other players to compete on the team. For Justin Upton, it was an eye-opening experience, but it also gave him continued confidence.

"I was on the team. At that point, there was no point in me really playing much. Those guys were all very close to college and getting drafted, and I was only going into ninth grade. It is a big jump from Freshman to those who were Juniors and Seniors. I wasn't as strong as those guys, but I think I started to turn a corner, and I began to develop it at that point. A lot of that was from being around them and trying to play at that level with them. I was younger, not as strong, maybe not as fast, and it pushed me," said Justin Upton.

Justin Upton had nothing to compare the group in terms of thinking of the players' professional prospects, but he knew they were good.

"I didn't know what a major leaguer would look like at that age. I was only 13 or 14, but I think those guys were very elite for that age, their mannerisms on the field, their skill level. I knew they were some of the best players I had ever seen at the time," Justin Upton.

"Lee Banks was able to get the best players together, all on the same team, and put them in the best position to be seen and perform. He is probably one of the best doing it. He's done it for a long time," explained Justin Upton. "Lee Banks was able to attract the best talent and have them have fun playing together. It made it a cohesive group. It had to be hard for the coach with players from different school teams to play together on a team of mixed product guys. Lee

Banks made it fun for those guys, and I think ultimately that's what allowed them to have their best skills come out," said Justin Upton.

Michael Cuddyer and David Wright shared the field for the World Series. In All-Star games, David Wright competed with and against Justin Upton, Michael Cuddyer, and Ryan Zimmerman. Four of the Splendid 6 played in the World Series: Ryan Zimmerman, David Wright, B.J. Upton, and Michael Cuddyer. Ryan Zimmerman is the only one who could flash a World Series Championship as a flex during times they now meet up. But it is probably not in Ryan Zimmerman's nature to flex it, maybe just subtly knock it on the table every now and then.

The Splendid 6 are not the kind of people to brag about their accomplishments as baseball players. They were just boys living in the same area and shared a sports passion. Baseball was one of them, and they didn't really know how good they actually were or what they would eventually accomplish as ballplayers.

"I guess at the time you don't know that you have Mark Reynolds and Ryan Zimmerman and B.J. Upton on your team or to compete against," said David Wright. "I never knew we'd have the careers we had. If you told me back then we would be in the Major Leagues, I would say you were crazy," David Wright explained.

For David Wright, it was always one at a time, Little League, travel ball, high school ball, and then college and baseball there if possible.

"I didn't actually think about being a Major Leaguer. But, from the get-go, I wanted to help my parents pay for college, and I wanted to play Atlantic Coast Conference Baseball," said David Wright.

Players and parents did not have developed social media; texting and cell phones were still in their mainstream infancy.

Communications with interested Major League teams were usually through telephone landlines and the old-fashioned home and field visits. Outlets like ESPN and Baseball America now have Draft Rankings trying to project the build and frames for high school players. High school and college players are pegged for their future stardom and debated on which team is selecting them. Some baseball players have a national following before they are even in high school. Bryce Harper was put on the cover of *Sports Illustrated* at 16 with an article by Tom Verducci calling him the most exciting sports prodigy since LeBron James.

Placing a high school baseball player on their cover was a risky move for *Sports Illustrated*, which previously did not have such a happy baseball ending.

In 1989, *Sports Illustrated* placed Jon Peters on the cover with "SUPERKID" as the headline. Jon Peters was an excellent pitcher in Texas high school baseball, going 51-0. Peters lost the next start after being the first high school baseball player on the cover of Sports Illustrated. Peters took a college scholarship to Texas A&M. Arm injuries ended his college and baseball career by the time he was 21.

Just because you are hyped and anointed for superstardom in high school, college, or Major League Baseball does not guarantee the result. David Wright and his family always had the main plan of college and playing baseball at Georgia Tech. A Major League Baseball team would have to take David Wright in a high-enough draft slot to convince him not to play baseball in the Atlantic Coast Conference at Georgia Tech.

"Some teams would call and ask about taking first-round money, and the answer was obviously "of course," and there were some teams that call saying do you think you would take 10th or

12th round money," said David Wright. "I didn't know where teams had me high on their list until I was actually drafted. I thought I was set with going to school at Georgia Tech. I never knew how I stacked up to other players until I played in national tournaments that I did well in. But I never knew how I stacked up against kids from Texas or Florida or California," explained David Wright.

If one of the Splendid 6 is asked to name which was the best baseball player as a kid, most will try to deflect from themselves. If pressed, however, the competitive nature of sports bred on those Hampton Roads fields of hard dirt and long outfield grass bubble to the surface. But David Wright had the benefit of size to the other players, with the other players growing into themselves later on.

"I, of course, say me. I would say I was big. I matured more quickly than those other guys did. I could always remember being a little bigger than them, and I was a chubbier kid. I was bigger and stronger than them at the same age. I think it taught me at a young age of the importance of discipline," said David Wright.

Rhon Wright did not run a fitness boot camp on David, but anytime David wanted to run with him, Rhon happily spent the time and effort with him. Exercise and fitness were essential to Rhon as a Police Officer, and they became essential to David as well.

"My dad and I are the same way; my dad can gain and lose weight. He has a crazy amount of discipline when it comes to dieting, but he also will binge junk food with the best of them, gain like 10 or 15 pounds, and then lose the weight two weeks later. So, I learned at a young age to be careful because I could do the same thing. I wanted to steal bases, and I wanted to play shortstop and be quick," explained David Wright.

I could hear what other people were saying about my weight. Coach Erbe's got a great story. We're playing some team at a national tournament, and the coach went up to him and told him, I was a little pudgy and they were going to try and hit it toward the pudgy shortstop. Coach Erbe came back with he hopes he does," laughed David Wright.

"But I knew bigger shortstops could play in the Major Leagues. Cal Ripken, Jr. wasn't pudgy by any stretch, but he was a bigger shortstop. Each year as a child, we would try to go to Camden Yards. We would sit in the nosebleeds. Cal Ripken was my idol because he was a bigger shortstop, and I was a bigger shortstop," explained David Wright. "I couldn't get crazy big, but I could tell at a young age that I was bigger than a lot of other kids, a little chubbier than a lot of other kids. I needed to be self-aware of it, but I wasn't going to let it restrict me for what position I could play or what I wanted to do on the baseball field," said David Wright.

David Wright knew, however, that he was not the best at all the skills in baseball with the Showcase Mets team.

"B.J. always was the most athletic. He could jump higher than all of us, run faster, a lot quicker. Ryan was the best defender of the group. I always remember taking groundballs these like kind of contests with him. He always had great hands, and I was just trying to keep up with him. He was shorter than me and much skinnier than me. He went to the University of Virginia and became one of the best college players in the Nation. Zimmerman had a slighter frame, but when he got drafted, I saw him, he had sprouted up and filled out quick and had a different body style than when we were in high school," said David Wright.

Another one of the players was super skinny and went to the University of Virginia. Reynolds was the only one of the Splendid 6 to not be a First-Rounder but showed immense Major League power and was the leader for the Splendid 6 in home runs for a season.

"Mark Reynolds kind of fell behind in the draft process, but he made it pretty quick, and he had a great career. Fast forward a couple of years into the big leagues, and he clearly had the most power of the group of us. You could tell in high school everything with him was just like really good. There wasn't like one thing that kind of stuck out. He was really good, and then he went to the University of Virginia and got even better. Obviously, he had, you know, power, more power than probably any one of us. Once he settled in, though, he possessed 'light-tower power.' It was amazing," explained David Wright.

Mark Reynolds changed his game from his travel and high school teams. "He began to go for the bombs and deployed a huge and powerful swing, resulting in tape-measure home runs and lots of strikeouts. His batting practice sessions were something to enjoy," said David Wright.

Mark Reynolds would launch batting practice home runs with one of his Splendid 6 teammates peeking from the dugout tunnel when they would play a season series against each other. Reynolds never knew of his baseball spy until he was interviewed for this book. The moment was a surprise and source of pride from Mark Reynolds.

"I used to sneak out and watch him hit batting practice. I did this to watch maybe three guys on opposing teams my whole career: Albert Pujols, Barry Bonds, and Mark Reynolds. Those three were just jaw-dropping when they hit," said David Wright.

By the time Wright, Reynolds, Zimmerman, and the Upton Brothers came together to play for the Lee Banks Showcase Mets

Travel Team, it was the first and only time they played on the same team or on the same field at the same time.

The Blasters and the Drillers were organizations with different teams and playing schedules. The players were in such a local and condensed area that their baseball diamonds crossed, but they never could truly practice and compete together or against each other simultaneously.

Lee Banks changed all that for them and gave them a baseball education in teamwork, cooperation, and how it would feel to be on a team where you looked to the left and right of you with a player better or equal to you.

"All of us were competitive. I think what made us all big leaguers was fierce competitiveness. Banks facilitated, but he was like the general manager, and he put together the best kids in the area. Banks could coach, but I think he enjoyed more putting the roster together and setting up the tournaments against the other better teams," said David Wright.

Of course, a showcase team is different in many ways for the players. High school ball for them was about to win as a team, not to highlight one particular player, and the high school games are not put on for scouts and college coaches as the primary audience. Showcase teams for these high school upperclassmen were all about being seen and noticed in the best possible light and at the position that showed their best potential for the next level. Wright, Reynolds, Zimmerman, and the Upton Brothers played the same position. The shortstop was not a weakness on the roster.

"Banks was responsible for getting many scouts and college coaches to come to our games. He would hype us to them up and say,

"Hey, look, we got this kid," and would be "he would be great for your program" or be "great for pro ball," explained David Wright.

Coach Lee Banks knew Justin Upton all the way from when the player was a Bat Boy and reserve player on the David Wright and B.J. Upton 12U Blasters Team. Coach Lee Banks had four First-Round picks, and a player who hit almost 300 MLB Home Runs to rotate in the lineup, all used to being the man and the shortstop for their respective teams.

Although Justin Upton was often the baby of the group, his baseball talent was not undersized, especially as the lens of time stretches into the 2020s, with the other Splendid 6 retiring by that point. Justin Upton continued the path the others started in front of him and easily leads the Splendid 6 in most offensive numbers.

Coach Lee Banks knew Justin Upton, and the Splendid 6 were ready to excel in baseball. Skills are obvious, but how to handle failing is a skill all baseball players need. The ability to concentrate on the most crucial opportunity: the next one.

"Baseball is a game of failure; those players knew that and dealt with it. Now you see some kids crying in the dugout; it's like get yourself together. Justin would strike out and then drill the next at-bat off the wall for a double. He just wanted his next at-bat to be better. They were just a special group of players," said Lee Banks.

Lee Banks never had to worry. The players were ready to play and make them all look good for the scouts at the Showcases.

"I just tried to not screw them up," said Lee Banks. There is still baseball left for the group. "I think Justin still has a few good years left and will surprise people," explained Lee Banks.

The baseball players started as kids barely able to hold a bat or throw a ball during Towny Townsend and Gary Lavelle camps. Then, they came up and through the same fields and the same people teaching them. Scouts and coaches were now looking at the same kids wanting to draft them or sign a scholarship.

Towny Townsend and his protégés had a secret sauce to help make kids better, both at sports and for adulthood, and to help shape so many lives. The man who batted under .200 with 0 HRS across two Minor League Seasons was developing the framework, passion, and the right coaches to help launch the Splendid 6. These players and dozens of others were about to dominate in the AAU, high school, college, Minor, and Major League fields for decades to follow.

Michael Cuddyer, David Wright, B.J. Upton, Justin Upton, Ryan Zimmerman, and Mark Reynolds rung up 8,370 Major League games played, 35,420 At-Bats, 9,436 Base Hits, 1,509 Home Runs, and 5,282 Runs-Batted-In across 85 Major League seasons. Also 15 All-Star appearances, 3 Gold Gloves, and a World Series Champion. As of 2022 Justin Upton is still playing.

Perhaps most impressively, all six of the players were prepared academically and athletically to such a high standard to be offered scholarships, drafted in the MLB Draft out of high school, or chose to play baseball in college.

Michael Cuddyer committed to Florida State before turning pro after being drafted 9th overall in the MLB Draft. Ryan Zimmerman and Mark Reynolds both committed and played at the University of Virginia. David Wright committed to Georgia Tech before being drafted 38th overall in the 2001 MLB Draft. B.J. Upton committed to Florida State before being drafted #2 overall in the 2002 MLB Draft. Before being drafted #1 in the 2003 MLB Draft, Justin Upton committed to North Carolina State. The Upton brothers are the only brothers to be #1 and #2 overall draft picks (in separate years).

EIGHTEEN:
DAVID WRIGHT

Towny Townsend's Hitting Discs were a part of David Wright's hitting routine up through his career. However, the actual basis of the Towny's Disc may also be a way to keep baseball a game and the reminders of a simple time of playing baseball. According to Sean Townsend, when David Wright went into the Minor Leagues, he just thought everybody used them and was surprised when he didn't see them.

"The Cool Whip lids were awesome. I was ultra-competitive, and it was always a game to me. It was always in a competition like winning a piece of gum if you hit the most in a row. When you're eight years old, a piece of gum might as well be a $00 bill. I was going to do everything I could to win," said David Wright.

"Kudos to Coach Towny because you have to have the talent to know how to sling them like Frisbees. He would sling them straight, and then, after a few minutes, make them move and then put some little curvatures, make it go like a breaking ball, or take you the opposite way like a screwball. It got my competitive juices flowing, and it helped my hand-eye coordination to hit this tiny little thin thing and made the baseball look so much bigger," explained David Wright.

"The Cool Whip hitting discs would wear out in time, the inside would fall out. The kids would put them on their heads and place their hat over them. It became a "Power Ring." When you are 12, you think it works," laughed Sean Townsend. With years to reflect on the discs, Sean Townsend knows there is more to the disc than improving bat lag and focus.

"The magic of the lid was not just in the lid; it was my father. He just made it fun," said Sean Townsend. The fun, though, was a competitive point of pride for the players on most lids in a row before swinging empty. "Jacob Dempsey hit 83 in a row of the lids for the record," said Sean Townsend.

Coach Allan Erbe knew David Wright's swing in and out as David was about to make the difficult choice between Pro and College ball. But even Coach Erbe, David Wright's perhaps longest and proudest non-family fan, could not accurately predict the depth and quality of David Wright's top performance levels.

Coach Erbe knows how to scout and project talent, and as a former associate scout for the Los Angeles Dodgers and Chicago Cubs he had his own assessment of David Wright as a player about to be drafted.

"When David was coming up, I told Major League baseball scouts he is going to be a .300 hitter, doubles and triples gap guy. Ten to 15 home runs per year. He is not going to be a 30 to 40 home run guy. He had more power than I thought he would have in the Major Leagues. I was wrong. He did hit a lot of doubles and triples, though. It is always tough to project power before they are fully mature. People thought David wasn't fast, but he had 20-20 seasons and even a 30-30 season for the Mets. David had a pretty average running speed for a Major Leaguer. David stole many of his bases on pitchers and on good jumps, like when he knew a curveball was coming. David wasn't Lou Brock, wasn't a Vince Coleman, but to steal third base in the Major Leagues, you have to have some speed," said Erbe.

David Wright was born on December 20, 1982. Hickory High School, School Body Vice-President. "Captain America" was Named the Gatorade Virginia High School Player of the Year in 2001...Also garnered Virginia All-State Player of the Year honors in 2001. Earned All-State honors in 1999, 2000, and 2001. Batted .538, with six home runs and 19 RBI his senior year. Over his four-year career at Hickory, he hit .438 with 13 home runs and 90 RBI. Born in Norfolk, Virginia, to a Police Officer, Rhon, and Elisa, a School Employee. Married Molly Beers in 2013 and has two daughters and a son. Committed to Georgia Tech before being drafted by the Mets.

"David Wright was an outstanding worker, who developed into a good power guy, always a good hitter. He developed from a pudgy young kid and worked hard to get in good shape and made himself into a great player," said Gary Lavelle.

Gary Lavelle was a coach and followed David Wright up-close from an opposing coach's view. "When I was coaching in Double-A, he was in the Minor Leagues, and I could just see he had Major

League talent written all over him. He was a grinder, always doing extra stuff like Michael Cuddyer," explained Gary Lavelle.

Supplemental first-round analysis by John Sickels of ESPN of the 2001 Results.

38. New York (N.L.)—David Wright, 3B, Hickory HS, Chesapeake, Va.

One of the best high school hitters in the Draft, Wright has good power to all fields, controls the strike zone, and impresses scouts with his work ethic and defensive skills at third base. He'll have to be bought away from Georgia Tech, but the Mets have the money. Wright isn't as "toolsy" as some of the guys picked ahead of him, but he is a better overall baseball player than many of them and could wind up being a steal in this slot.

Baseball America has this Scouting Report of Wright after the 2001 MLB Draft.

Drafted in the supplemental 1st round (38th overall) by the New York Mets in 2001 (signed for $960,000).

Wright has been compared to Michael Cuddyer, a fellow Tidewater product who was the ninth overall pick in the 1997 draft. Both have excellent makeup and work ethic, qualities that endear them to scouts. Their tools are similar, though Wright swings the bat a little better and has better overall mechanics at this age. If Wright were a little bigger and projected better, he'd be a candidate for the first 10 picks. Few players in the country swing the bat as well. Wright has developed more extension with his swing, giving him more power, but he still projects just 20 home runs a year in the big leagues. That's a marginal output by today's third-base standards, though he has settled in nicely at the position. He's at the heart of a strong Georgia Tech recruiting class.

College won't be an issue if he's drafted in the first 30-50 picks, where he's projected.

David Wright Career Highlights

- Only third player to play entire career for Mets
- Fourth player to be named Captain in Met's franchise history
- 7-time NL All-Star (2006–2010, 2012 & 2013)
- 2-time NL Gold Glove Winner (2007 & 2008)
- 2-time Silver Slugger Winner (2007 & 2008)
- 20-Home Run Seasons: 6 (2005–2008, 2010 & 2012)
- 30-Home Run Seasons: 2 (2007 & 2008)
- 100 Runs Scored Seasons: 2 (2007 & 2008)
- 100 RBI Seasons: 5 (2005–2008 & 2010)
- Earned the nickname of "Captain America" during his 2nd World Baseball Classic and only U.S. player named to the all-tournament team

Interesting playing facts on David Wright and perhaps why he should be enshrined in the Baseball Hall of Fame, despite his career being short and not able to compile many of the milestone statistics carried by other third baseman presently enshrined.

Wright, Ramirez, Howard Johnson, and Tommy Harper (1970) are the only third basemen in the 30-30 club in MLB history.

Wright had five seasons with 25-plus home runs, 15-plus stolen bases, and 100-plus RBIs. That's tied with Alex Rodriguez for the most such seasons by a third baseman in MLB history. No other third baseman has had more than two (Chipper Jones, Mike Schmidt, and Howard Johnson).

Only six players at any position in baseball history have had more of those 25/15/100 seasons than Wright. Rodriguez (11 total), Barry Bonds (eight), Beltran (six), Jose Canseco (six), Hank Aaron (six), and Willie Mays (six). Wright is tied with two other players at five: Jeff Bagwell and Ken Griffey, Jr.

As time goes on, David, his wife, and children spend more time in the California home and less time in their Chesapeake home. David Wright helped raise millions of dollars for the local Children's Hospital, Children's Hospital of Kings' Daughters. David Wright turned community service projects to benefit CHKD to the still playing and rising All-Star Los Angeles Dodger, Chris Taylor. Taylor was a member of the Drillers and is proud to pick up where David handed off.

"Chris is now doing a couple big fundraisers a year for the hospital. As I am getting older, I am proud to pass the torch to the younger kid. He is doing some excellent things for the area," said David Wright.

NINETEEN:
RYAN ZIMMERMAN

When I talked to Matt Sinnen and Gary Wright about the Drillers and their teams throughout the years, the first words out were their respect for Coach Towny Townsend and what the Blasters did. Still, it quickly and fairly went to the fact the Drillers produced three World Series Champions in Ryan Zimmerman, Daniel Hudson, and Chris Taylor. We all dig Rings.

Matt Sinnen, the life-long friend and protégée of Towny Townsend, could be a glimpse of what Coach Towny Townsend may have become had he not lost his battle with cancer. Matt Sinnen is over six feet tall, still fit and trim for a man in his early sixties and getting close to the full retirement age of Social Security benefits. But it is clear the messages of Towny Townsend are still alive today through Matt Sinnen, and he made his own way in baseball and evident pride in the players he produced.

Matt Sinnen has a contradictory voice full of a soothing bass, the skill of a storyteller, and the patience of a Pastor. That's why when he offered to help me get in touch with Ryan Zimmerman and Chris Taylor, I knew he was more than just proud of his players, he still cared for them, and they still cared for him. As much as David Wright meant to the Blasters, it was clear that Ryan Zimmerman was the same for the Drillers. "Zim is a great guy; he will be happy to talk to you. I will talk to him and get it going for you," said Matt Sinnen. By the next day, I had an email from Mr. National and Mr. Blaster offering to be interviewed.

As the day the interview was coming up, I was nervous because of big things in the Zimmerman's life. They were expecting another baby within days, the MLB Lockout was in dark days, and he still hadn't announced his intentions of playing or retiring. But when my cell rang, it was Ryan Zimmerman, and he sounded happy, content, and with a genuine enthusiasm to peel back some years and even reflect on his years ahead. But in the course of the phone call, we had an old score to settle. One that bothered me and was a source of one of his best favorite baseball moments.

Ryan Zimmerman gave me the closure he didn't know was so badly needed, by acknowledging he broke my heart as a Yankee fan in attendance at his extra-inning home run Father's Day game. Ryan Zimmerman said it was one of his favorite memories of his career as I remember not being happy with the young third baseman and dreaming up ways Brian Cashman could trade for him as I walked to a train back home to Maryland. I guess we can agree to disagree. However, I felt better getting that grudge out of the way with him directly.

The echoes of Towny Townsend and Matt Sinnen reverberated through our conversation.

"I think at some point everyone should try and give back," said Ryan Zimmerman. "We were lucky to have the coaching, instruction, and an influence on us at such a young age to be good men and to be good people. It only seems right at some point in my life to do the same thing," explained Ryan Zimmerman on some of his way forward for his other 80% and non-baseball playing portion.

Being a parent can change or reinforce what you think you knew about childhood or what you believe mentors or parents are, and all the paths are taken to get there.

"Thank you to the parents, the coaches. Being a parent now, I see the time commitment, I see the sacrifices me and my wife make with our kids; they are barely doing anything, so I can't imagine the sacrifices that my parents made. My brother is two and a half years younger than me and was involved in a lot of stuff too," explained Ryan Zimmerman.

Ryan Zimmerman thinks the Splendid 6 had talents but needed help from parents, coaches, and others to make it possible.

"I realize now how awesome parents are, what they did, what they sacrificed. There is a zero percent chance any of us would be in the situation without them. The same can be said for the coaches and other people. The amount of sweat, time, and sacrifice all these people put in to give us the luxuries and the ability to do what we did when we were those ages. I can't say thank you enough and more importantly, thank you for teaching us how to do things the right way and how to be good people," said Ryan Zimmerman.

Ryan Zimmerman, Mr. Driller, is perhaps the most accomplished and decorated player from the Drillers Organization.

However, a protégé upstaged his mentor and was able to grab a future World Champion. Matt Sinnen beat Towny Townsend to scoop up, who many believe had the best hands to be produced during the Hampton Roads glory days and boom of baseball.

"I had the absolute pleasure and honor of coaching Ryan Zimmerman with his father for nine years. It was just fun to watch that kid practice. I could tell watching him for the first time as a 10-year-old that he had a future in baseball," said Matt Sinnen.

Like a scene from "Back to the Future" when the band calls a producer and excitedly claims to see the next big thing, Sinnen called Gary Wright to take a look at Zimmerman.

"He actually reminded me a lot of Towny. He just did things differently. He was already diving for balls, running balls down, and catching them over his head at that age. He was a tall, lengthy, and scrawny kid athletically. Ryan was the least athletic of the five by a large margin at that age, but Ryan had the IT factor. Better hands than anyone ever to come out of this area. Ryan has these gifts from God, his hands and his instinct before the ball was pitched, he got that extra step from somewhere," said Matt Sinnen.

Coaches can be loyal to their players' core long after they are their coach. In New York City's baseball heyday during the 1950s, managers and fans alike would debate the best center fielder from the choice of Willie May, Duke Snider, and Mickey Mantle. The Giants, Dodgers, and Yankees fans were always right in their belief. It is a beautiful part of baseball. And we all know Mick was the best of the three.

The Wright-versus-Zimmerman debate is part of that time-honored give and take. Some in Hampton Roads could even say Towny would have given Zimmerman and Wright a good run at defense if times were different after he punched out his manager.

Coaches and teammates like Matt Sinnen and Mark Reynolds have their own take on the Wright or Zimmerman best third base glove debate.

"Dave may have been a cornerstone for the Mets at third base; I saw Zim so much in college, I saw plays, while I was just feet away, from Zimmerman that were absolutely amazing, so I give the glove to Zimmerman over David," said Mark Reynolds.

"Zimmerman was a better fielder than David Wright at third. I know David probably has more Gold Gloves than Ryan, and those two can have their own argument. One played in New York, one played in Washington. Wright was ahead of him in the big leagues and had already won some awards," explained Matt Sinnen. "It is hard to replace the incumbent. No matter what the award says, David hitting 35 home runs a year and .300 each year is part of the Gold Gloves. I'm biased, but I don't think anybody in the area would tell you they saw better hands and throws than Zimmerman. Ryan is the greatest infielder ever to come out of our area," said Matt Sinnen.

> *He is the epitome of a lead-by-example guy. If I said it once, I said it a million times to the other younger players: "Just watch the way he prepares." He is not verbose. He doesn't have to scream and yell to get his point across. It all starts with performance on the field, but it also trickles in to respect in the clubhouse, what he does in the community with his foundation and that sort of thing.*
>
> – Washington Nationals General Manager Mike Rizzo on MLB.com (Bill Ladson, 02/26/2012)

Ryan Zimmerman was born on September 28, 1984. Kallam High School in Virginia Beach. Played college ball at the University of Virginia. "Mr. National," the Washington National's first-ever Draft Pick at 4th overall (2005). A third baseman and first baseman. As the baseball Lockout dragged on, Ryan Zimmerman retired before the 2022 baseball season. A .277 batting average, 284 home runs, and 1,061 RBI for his career.

Scouting Report filed by Baseball America upon Ryan Zimmerman's Draft Selection.

Drafted in the 1st round (4th overall) by the Washington Nationals in 2005 (signed for $2,975,000).

Zimmerman played second base for a high school summer team that featured B.J. Upton at shortstop and David Wright at third base, but he went undrafted out of high school. Teams won't miss out on the opportunity this time around. His bat control and elite defensive ability have the Royals and Expos targeting Zimmerman, and his polish could give them a quick return on that investment. His professional stock soared. Last summer, he earned MVP honors at the World University Championship, leading Team USA to a gold medal in Taiwan while setting a USA Baseball record with a .468 average. Even more impressive to scouts were his team-best numbers in home runs (four) and RBIs (27) with wood bats. That allayed concerns about a lack of power after he finished with only one home run for Virginia in 2004, though he always has shown gap power. He was among the Atlantic Coast Conference batting leaders again this season and had six home runs. Zimmerman rarely strikes out because of his balanced, up-the-middle approach and shows average speed and good instincts on the basepaths. He's always had excellent defensive skills, with hands, feet, arm strength, and range that all rate above average. He has even played at least a dozen games at shortstop for Virginia, allowing the Cavaliers to get more offense in the lineup, and a pro club might try him in the middle infield. One scout called him the best defender he had ever seen—at any position—and said the only question about Zimmerman was how many Gold Gloves he would win. His makeup also gets high marks; he returned from his strong summer playing with the intensity of a walk-on.

- 2004 USA Baseball National Team, winning the gold medal and MVP in the FISU II World University Baseball Championship
- 2006 Topps All-Star Rookie Team
- 2-time NL All-Star (2009 & 2017)
- NL Gold Glove Winner (2009/3B)
- 2-time NL Silver Slugger Award Winner (2009 & 2010/3B)
- 20-Home Run Seasons: 7 (2006, 2007, 2009, 2010, 2012, 2013 & 2017)
- 30-Home Run Seasons: 2 (2009 & 2017)
- 100 RBI Seasons: 3 (2006, 2009 & 2017)
- 100 Runs Scored Seasons: 1 (2009)
- World Series Championship with the Washington Nationals in 2019

Zimmerman's mother, Cheryl, was diagnosed with multiple sclerosis in 1995, needing a wheelchair since 2000. Zimmerman founded the ziMS Foundation, dedicated to treating and curing multiple sclerosis. Zimmerman became engaged to Heather Downen, a tech-firm sales representative, in April 2012. They married in January 2013. The couple has four children as of January 2022.

TWENTY:
B.J. UPTON

Racism in the United States of America is a thorny and raw issue to discuss. Talking about racism and baseball had to be difficult discussing with a young African American baseball player poised to be a First Round Draft pick. Still, Coach Townsend told him the ins and outs he endured as an Italian with a Catholic upbringing while playing in places like the Carolinas.

Coach Towny Townsend knew B.J. Upton would face racism and stereotypes in the Minor Leagues, and did the best he could to ensure B.J. Upton would handle racism better than he did himself as a young Boston Red Sox farmhand. Towny talked with B.J. Upton about the racial incident that put his dream to play for the Boston Red Sox in the ground.

"Coach T's story is one of the stories that never left my brain. I knew right then, I'm like Hell, this is a white man telling me this, and here I am about to get drafted, and there's a good chance that I'm going somewhere in the South. It was something that I've never forgotten, even to this day. It affected me 100%. I played in Charleston, Montgomery, and Durham, and some of the places that I've been to play on the road; it's like yeah, it goes on, it happens. It can even happen from somebody wearing the same uniform as you. I think that's what shocked me the most. In high school, you're still kids, and we're playing the team game, we're in this together, and then I think it made me realize there are grown men in this, I mean I hate to say it, but it's pretty much every man for himself," said B.J. Upton.

Virginia is considered part of the traditional South, with the Capitol of the Confederacy in Richmond, but living in the Coastal Virginia area did not really prepare B.J. Upton for some of the issues he later experienced.

"Coastal Virginia, it's still pretty South, but I didn't have those problems growing up in Virginia. Can I say I dealt with none of it? I'd be lying if I said that, but I was very fortunate given the circumstances. In the community I grew up in, we all loved each other. There might have been a few, but there were very few, but we all loved each other. To me, it just goes to say a lot about the people where I'm from, especially the Great Bridge Hickory area."

Black athletes choosing to play baseball have become rarer and more difficult in a region with so many African Americans choosing to play basketball and football.

"I always got joked on about wanting to play baseball. It happened all the time by my guys on my AAU basketball team and from the football guys. 'Man, why are you playing baseball.' To be honest,

I heard a lot of times, 'It's the white boy's game.' It didn't bother me, I've seen some of those same guys later, and they told me, 'Damn bro, we should have played baseball with you,'" said B.J. Upton.

B.J. Upton never had any problems with racism with the Blasters. His high school baseball time was a somewhat different experience for him, though.

"I had more problems with the guys on my high school team. I didn't even play varsity my freshman year, and there were some guys on that team that were racist."

B.J. Upton later transferred to be play baseball at Greenbriar Christian Academy with Coach Towny Townsend.

"My dad always said there are plenty of kids with talent, African American kids, and nobody wants to teach them," said B.J. Upton. "I don't know why it happens," explained B.J. Upton.

Major League scouts will usually drive anywhere to just get a peek at a promising player. Baseball scouts are deployed across the globe to get valuable information, eyes on a player, and maybe build a relationship to sign players. But perhaps some of the best athletes in America are not being earnestly pursued, or scouts just rely on large baseball travel showcases and eschew other all-round athletes or players whose parents cannot finance a travel baseball lifestyle.

"It blows my mind that they will go into—and I'm talking about Major League scouts—would rather go into a third-world country than into a neighborhood that might not be so good to go see a kid who's right here on their own soil. They will go to the Dominican Republic, Venezuela, and we're starting to see more Colombian players in the league now; they'll go there but won't go into this neighborhood to see this kid because his neighborhood and school might not be that good. It's not fair, and it's been going on for years," said B.J. Upton.

The pace of other professional sports to bigger contracts and no vast farm systems are part of the pull away from Major League Baseball for some players.

"Part of it is baseball and the minor leagues. In other leagues, like the NBA, you can go to college basketball for one year and come out. Football, you may have to wait, but we see that's changing. It's more instant money with the other two leagues than it is baseball, even with the baseball signing bonus," explained B.J. Upton.

"We see the football players and the basketball players. We see LeBron James in commercials all the time. I don't know any baseball commercials on repeat right now. I don't know why, but if African American players were advertised more, it would help. I just don't think the advertising is there. The little number of guys in baseball need to be advertised to bring awareness to it," said B.J. Upton.

B.J. Upton is proud he and his brother are African American baseball players picked in the First Round. Both are examples of African American players making it in the Major Leagues, and perhaps could lead to more African American ballplayers coming up. However, visibility and the marketing of African American players are needed to draw further interest. In addition, youth coaches need to be more willing to do the outreach to show that baseball is another option as a sport and fun to play.

"We always said we hope to be an example for other kids, especially other African American kids. Talent must meet coaching; the opportunity must be there. I just don't see kids in inner cities or African American kids gravitating toward baseball. It is the job of the African American players in the Big Leagues right now to be seen and to do our best to have kids gravitate toward the game. I think they'll be put in positions where we can talk about the game and be more visible over time. The kids will find the coaching and can play at the college level and then maybe further their careers," said B.J. Upton.

B.J. Upton had all five tools, was a great pitcher in High School who touched 94 mph. Could have been whatever he wanted and still been a top-round draft pick. He could make any team he was on really good, said Gary Lavelle on how B.J. Upton appeared as a high school player.

Melvin "B.J." Upton was born on August 21, 1984. Upton graduated from Greenbriar Christian Academy. Mother Yvonne was a teacher, and Father Melvin was a Scout for Kansas City Royals and a mortgage broker. In 2002, Upton was named a first-team All-American by Baseball America, batting .641 (50-for-78) with 11 doubles, 4 triples, 11 home runs, and 32 RBI during his senior year at Greenbrier. B.J. Upton hit .633 with 13 home runs, 51 RBI, 44 runs, and 43 stolen bases in 47 attempts during his high school career. He signed a letter of intent to play college baseball at Florida State before ultimately signing with the Tampa Rays after being selected with the second overall pick in the 2002 Regular Season Draft. During his career, B.J. Upton hit 164 home runs and 586 Runs Batted In. B.J. is a brother with Major League Baseball player Justin Upton.

- 20-home run seasons: 4 (2007, 2011, 2012 & 2016)
- Four 20-20 seasons (at least) 20 H.R. and 20 S.B. during the season
- 300 career stolen bases

- Three straight 40 stolen base seasons (2008-2010)
- Part of 5 postseason teams, including the 2008 World Series with Tampa Bay Rays

There have been 350 sets of brothers in MLB History. However, only six brother tandems have each hit at least 100 home runs. Brothers with 100+ career home runs each:

#1. 488. B.J. Upton (168) and Justin Upton (324)

#2. 486. Joe DiMaggio (363) and Vince DiMaggio (125)

#3. 444. Ken Boyer (282) and Clete Boyer (162)

#4. 378. Brett Boone (252) and Aaron Boone (126)

#5. 322. Roberto Alomar (210) and Sandy Alomar, Jr. (112)

#6. 262. Bob Meusel (156) and Irish Meusel (106)

B.J. needs Justin to hit 280 more home runs to match the brother (regardless of a minimum of home run by a brother) duo of Hank (755) and Tommy (13) Aaron at 768.

If you count Dom DiMaggio to his brothers Joe and Vince, they stand at 573 home runs. Dom DiMaggio was a great player in his own right, with 87 career home runs, and 7 All-Star Games, despite three years lost to World War II military service.

The 2002 Scouting Report by Baseball America for the regular season draft:

Drafted in the 1st round (2nd overall) by the Tampa Bay Rays in 2002 (signed for $4,600,000).

Upton is the consensus top-ranked player in the Draft, even if the Pirates don't take him. He has the complete package. He's athletic, has all the tools, and is an exciting player to watch. And he's by far the best player at a premium position. On the standard 20-80 scouting scale, he has a 75-80 arm (he can throw 90 mph across the diamond and 92 off a mound) and 70 speed (he runs the 60 in 6.55 seconds). He has good hands and excellent first-step acceleration, which is evident in both fielding balls and running the bases. His range for a middle infielder is outstanding. The only questions concern his bat. He has a wiry build with a chance for power but needs to get stronger. Scouts compare Upton to a young Derek Jeter, right down to the swagger. Upton is further along in his development than Jeter at a comparable age. He's more physically mature than Jeter, who developed his physique in pro ball and has better power. Upton is just 17 and will play at that age throughout his first professional season. Scouts are curious how he'll handle the pressure of experiencing failure for the first time, since he's rarely failed at any step of his baseball career.

Fun Facts on B.J. Upton

- For most of his career, he was known by the nickname B.J., which stands for Bossman Junior; his father's nickname is Bossman.
- His younger brother Justin was the #1 overall pick in the 2005 draft by the Arizona Diamondbacks.
- B.J. and Justin are the only brothers to be selected #1 (Justin, 2005) and #2 (B.J., 2002) in the MLB Draft.
- Both brothers were drafted as shortstops but later moved to the outfield.
- B.J. and Justin became the first set of brothers to post 20-20 seasons the same year; they were already only the 6th set of brothers to have each had such a season.

- In both 2004 and 2005, Upton was the starting shortstop in the All-Star Futures Game.
- In 2009, B.J. Upton became the first Tampa Bay Ray to hit for a Cycle.
- On August 3, 2012, Upton hit his 100th career home run. Justin Upton hit his 100th career home run earlier the same day.
- In 2013, His brother Justin was acquired in a trade reuniting the Upton brothers. B.J. and Justin went back-to-back with home runs on April 23, which was the first-time brothers hit back-to-back home runs since Lloyd and Paul Warner did for the Pirates in 1938.
- In 2014, August 8, B.J. and Justin set a Major League record when they hit home a run in the same game for the fifth time, setting a new Major League record for brothers, passing Vladimir and Wilton Guerrero and Jason and Jeremy Giambi.

TWENTY-ONE:

JUSTIN UPTON

Justin Upton was probably the most talented of all of them. All Five tools, it just came easy to him.

– Gary Lavelle.

Justin Upton was born on August 25, 1987. Great Bridge High School in Chesapeake. Four-time All-Star 2009, 2011, 2015, and 2017. Selected #1 Overall on 2005 MLB Draft. Upton was an all-district shortstop for Great Bridge High School in Chesapeake, Virginia. He won the AFLAC National High School Player of the Year Award. Baseball America ranked him as the top high school baseball prospect. Upton verbally committed to play baseball at North Carolina State. Hit .417 for Team USA at the 2004 World Junior Championship. Drafted in the 1st round (1st overall) by the Arizona Diamondbacks in 2005 (signed for $6,100,000).

Justin Upton's Scouting Report on Baseball America before the 2005 Regular Season Draft

Upton stands as the favorite to become the draft's first overall pick, which would trump his brother B.J., whom the Devil Rays selected second in 2002. The sibling rivalry doesn't stop there. Justin has proven equally athletic and more advanced offensively than B.J. at the same age, demonstrating excellent patience at the plate and a quick stroke. Upton's well-defined and muscular upper body give a hint to his plus power potential, which he accompanies with equal amounts of speed. His 6.23-second time in the 60-yard dash at a Perfect Game showcase last year rates as the quickest in the scouting service's history. Upton moves well defensively and shows clean actions at Shortstop, but again follows in his brother's footsteps because he has trouble harnessing the plus arm strength that has allowed him to hit 94 mph off the mound. The throwing errors come from not maintaining consistent mechanics, a problem that fades when Upton long tosses or makes throws from the Outfield. This has led some scouts to profile him as a center fielder, though Upton would prefer to remain at Shortstop. He actually played third base late in his senior season, making all the plays thereafter switching positions with a teammate who struggled to make the long throws from the hot corner. Wherever Upton lands defensively, teams will buy the bat. His character and work ethic often go under-reported, as people tend to focus on the five-tool skills. He's handled the expectations of being tagged 2005's top prospect since his freshman year of high school with aplomb, routinely playing in front of scores of scouts and answering countless questions from scouts and media alike. He continues to back up the hype, with his performance at the World Junior Championship in September as a prime example. He led Team USA in runs (eight), hits (10), triples (four), total bases (21), and slugging (.875).

- In 2007, Upton hit .357 for the Diamondbacks in the postseason as they made it to the NLCS. Played that season with childhood friend and teammate Mark Reynolds.
- In 2009, Upton was named N.L. Player of the Month of May. His brother Melvin Upton, Jr. earned A.L. Player of the Month of June, making Justin and B.J. the first pair of brothers to win player of the month honors in the same year.
- In 2011, B.J. and Justin Upton became the first brothers to hit 20-20 in the same season.
- Upton was traded and reunited with his brother B.J. on the Atlanta Braves for the 2013 season.
- In 2013, B.J. and Justin went back-to-back with home runs on April 23, which was the first-time brothers hit back-to-back home runs since Lloyd and Paul Warner did for the Pirates in 1938.
- In 2014, B.J. and Justin set a Major League record when they hit home runs in the same game for the fifth time, setting a new Major League record for brothers, passing Vladimir and Wilton Guerrero and Jason and Jeremy Giambi.
- In 2021, The Upton Brothers passed Joe DiMaggio and Vince DiMaggio when Justin Upton hit his 323rd home run to combine with B.J. Upton's 168 home runs to pass the DiMaggio Brothers for the most Home Runs by two brothers, with each having at least 100 home runs.
- There have been 350 sets of brothers in MLB History. Only 6 brother tandems have each hit at least 100 home runs.

Notable Achievements:

- 4-time All-Star (2009, 2011, 2015 & 2017)
- 3-time Silver Slugger Award winner (2011/NL, 2014/NL & 2017/AL)
- 20-home run seasons: 8 (2009, 2011 & 2013-2018)
- 30-home run seasons: 4 (2011 & 2016-2018)
- 100 RBI seasons: 2 (2014 & 2017)
- 100 runs scored seasons: 3 (2011, 2012 & 2017)

TWENTY-TWO:
MARK REYNOLDS

Mark Reynolds is the first player I met of the Splendid 6. Mark and I have a common connection through a friend of mine. Mark Reynolds is the son-in-law of Bill and Vicki Shanahan. Yes, that Bill Shanahan, the Bill Shanahan.

Bill Shanahan loves to tell his version of the story of how his daughter Kathleen began dating Mark Reynolds. Bill Shanahan had a standing rule for his daughters: there was no dating of the baseball players on any of the teams he was involved with. An easy, clear, and concise directive from a father to his daughters. As a father of two daughters, I barely can restrain laughing at the thought of that working.

"After Mark made the Big Leagues, I got a call from Mark saying he had been talking some with Kathleen and he wanted to ask if he could date her since he had a rule on ballplayers," said Bill Shanahan. The phone call probably did not go as Mark Reynolds hoped it would.

"I hung up on him," said Bill Shanahan. "I instantly called Billy Butler, the manager of the Double-A team, and asked what kind of guy Mark was," explained Bill Shanahan. After that, they had Bill Shanahan's blessing. Now Mark and Kathleen are married with kids, the oldest of whom is 14.

When Justin Upton was told the Bill Shanahan version of the story, it was hard for him to believe. There may have been an alternative narrative and shiftable facts to the love story.

"Let's go with that story; that's a good one," laughed Justin Upton.

Mark Reynolds has interesting layers to the story open for some interpretation, but still shows Kathleen and Mark's respect for not upsetting Bill Shanahan.

I was out one night with some friends, and I ran into her; I liked her, and we began to talk. Eventually, she asked why I was in Mobile, and I said I was playing for the Bay Bears.

In what had to be a scene reminiscent of Casablanca, Kathleen's face broke out in an "Of all the gin joints in all the towns in the world, he walks into mine" face. But it seems not enough to deter young adults from forming a budding relationship.

"Once I made the Diamondbacks, I didn't want to keep things secret, and I would end things if I couldn't date her openly. I called her father. He hung up on me. But I guess he checked around on me and called me back later with his blessing to date Kathleen," said Mark Reynolds.

Bill Shanahan is closing in on his 40th-year professional sports ownership, management, and operations. Bill Shanahan has a Triple Crown as a baseball executive, winning the Executive of the Year honors in the Southern League (three times), California League in 1988, and the South Atlantic League in 1992. This man loves baseball and can discuss players ranging from Snuffy Stirnweiss to Willie Mays.

I first met Bill Shanahan when he and his wife Vicki migrated Blowfish across the Congaree River in South Carolina to form the Lexington County Blowfish in 2015. My wife Barbara and I hosted a young and funny pitcher from the University of Georgia, Blake Hamilton, that Summer. The role of a Host Family for the Lexington County Blowfish was a new way for us to enjoy baseball and led us to become Season Ticketholders.

I did not know Bill Shanahan at the time, but I would see a man a bit older than me, wearing slacks and a Blowfish polo, running circles past his college interns. Bill Shanahan is hard to slow down during a game, but if you mention a throwback baseball name like Bobby Richardson, years fall off his face and he begins to resemble a baseball Peter Pan.

Bill Shanahan and I became close friends over the years, and he first introduced me to Mark Reynolds, just after Mark Reynolds was finishing playing for his last Major League team. Don't forget, Mark Reynolds played with Derek Jeter and the New York Yankees. I was excited to shake the hand of someone who knew Derek Jeter. Our conversation on the Concourse was polite and brief as I awkwardly asked him about Derek Jeter. "Great guy and teammate," Mark

Reynolds said. Nothing more, just a couple of seconds of silence as the next Blowfish batter stepped in at the plate.

A brain bomb dropped internally, and I felt his baseball career or anything else about players he played with were not something he wanted to discuss at the time. I am guessing at the time he was trying to balance whether to keep grinding and find a spot on a Major League team or retire. Why else would someone not want to talk to someone they didn't know about someone they probably did not know that well? Right?

I would see Mark Reynolds occasionally and did not try to charge the baseball hill. In December of 2021, Mark Reynolds was the Featured Speaker at a Lexington County Blowfish Baseball Prayer Breakfast. He stood up and gave testimony on his relationship with God, the challenges of being a ballplayer, and the balance of family and baseball. There he was talking about baseball and sharing stories.

"He might want to talk baseball," I thought. I stood around waiting for people to talk or finish up with their selfies with him. I finally had a real Major Leaguer who would possibly talk baseball with me! I had to remind myself not to ask about the New York Yankees or Derek Jeter.

I mentioned what I knew of the Tidewater Baseball Boys. David Wright, Ryan Zimmerman, B.J. Upton, and himself, and how amazing it was to all come from the same area and play all those years on the same travel team. Mark Reynolds nodded and said that they only briefly played on a team together. It also included Justin Upton, and no mention of the Tidewater Baseball Boys was complete without Michael Cuddyer. Boom! I felt corrected, shamed, and energized.

Like that, Mark Reynolds gave me the inspiration to tell a version of the Tidewater Baseball Boys, a team of six kids who could outshine the "Van Buren Boys" gang of eight from a Seinfeld episode.

Baseball America's Scouting report on Mark Reynolds before 2004 Regular Season Draft.

Drafted in the 16th round (476th overall) by the Arizona Diamondbacks in 2004.

SS Mark Reynolds has good actions, with average arm strength and range, but most scouts think he will have to move to second base in pro ball. He is decent with the bat (.288-10-43) but has a slow trigger and tries to play a big man's game instead of playing to his strengths.

Mark Reynolds was born on August 3, 1983, played high school baseball at First Colonial High School. As a college freshman, Reynolds hit .283 with 15 home runs. Collegiate Baseball named him a freshman All-American. A 16th Round Pick in the 2004 MLB Draft out of the University of Virginia, where he was teammates with Ryan Zimmerman. His 35 career home runs at Virginia are tied for second all-time in Cavalier history.

- Owns a New York Yankees Franchise Record and tied for Major League Record by hitting a home run in his first at-bat for the Yankees and then a home run in his last at-bat for the Yankees.
- Led Towny's Boys with the most home runs in a Major League season with 42.
- Joined the 20-20 Club by hitting 44 home runs and stealing 24 bases.
- Nicknamed "Skeletor."

- His 10-RBI game on July 7, 2018, is rarer in Baseball than a Perfect Game.
- He is one of only a handful of players to hit 250 or more home runs and never make the MLB All-Star team.

I am definitely going to leave the field dirty. I am not afraid to dive into the stands; I am not afraid to take on a catcher at home plate. I definitely play the game 100 percent, full board all nine innings, and you'll never see me loafing out there. If I am loafing, it must mean that I am hurt. I am a hard-nosed player, and I'll go out there every day with all I've got.

– Mark Reynolds on MLB.com

Reynolds led MLB baseball with the Power-Speed number (PSN) of 31.1. PSN is a sabermetrics baseball statistic developed by baseball author and analyst Bill James, which combines a player's home run and stolen base numbers into one number. (It is the harmonic mean of the two totals.) James introduced the power-speed number writing, 'It is so crafted that a player who does well in both home runs and stolen bases will rate high, and his rating is determined by the balance of the two as well as by the total."

In 2011, Reynolds became the first player in the history of Oriole Park at Camden Yards to hit a home run into the 2nd Deck (Club Level) in Left Field. The shot was estimated at 463 feet.

In 2012, on September 6, Reynolds hit two home runs against the New York Yankees. It was only the second time since 1918 that a player had three multi-homer games against the Yankees in a single season.

In 2018, Reynolds reunited with childhood baseball teammate and opponent when he joined the Washington Nationals, Ryan Zimmerman. Reynolds hit two home runs in his first game as a Washington National. On July 7, Reynolds went 5-5 with two home runs, a double, and a career-high, franchise record-tying 10 RBIs.

Notable Achievements

- 20-home run seasons: 8 (2008-2014 & 2017)
- 30-home run seasons: 4 (2009-2011 & 2017)
- 40-home run seasons: 1 (2009)
- 100 RBI seasons: 1 (2009)
- 2009 June 14 N.L. Player of the Week
- 2009 August 9 N.L. Player of the Week
- 2010 April 25 N.L. Player of the Week
- 2018 July 8 N.L. Player of the Week

Mark Reynolds Quotes Too Good Not to Share

On the way, baseball was and should be: *Baseball is a tough sport; not everyone gets a trophy.*

On the coaching style of B.J. and Justin's Father, the original Boss Man, Manny Upton, Sr.: *Manny was an intense coach. For example, as a team at a National Tournament tried to dazzle us with an elaborate infield during warm-ups, he refused to have them try to intimidate us, so he told us all to turn our backs to the field at the same time.*

On taking a second or two to take a moment as he played with Justin Upton for the 2007 Arizona Diamondbacks: *I remember a time in Arizona with Justin, he was on-deck as the three-hitter, and I was in-the-hole as clean-up, and we just looked at each other and started laughing "like dude, how'd this happen?"*

On the privilege of playing for his Country and Team USA: *Playing for Team USA was a huge honor. I have very few framed items from my career, and my Team USA Jersey is one of them. It was a great honor during my career.*

On falling just short of the 300-Home Run Club at 298. Besides a World Series Championship, this player milestone still nags him at times: *I wish I hit a couple more home runs to get to 300.*

Thinking back at the Splendid 6 Tidewater Boys, their accomplishments, and why he thought it was possible: *We have so much accomplished through the years. It was no accident or coincidence it happened though with all the great coaches and the parents we had, and the fact that as players, we all pushed each other.*

Some of the differences coming up as a youth and in the Major Leagues: *As a Blaster, we worked on situational batting, and all about contact, but in the Major Leagues, it was about getting home runs.*

Explaining why he focused on power numbers and not worrying about striking out as much: *I could have done a bunch of things average in the Major Leagues, but when I concentrated on home runs, it helped me stand out.*

On his baseball focus now: *I'm grateful to help as a coach with my son's team. Some of the lessons I learned as a kid, I can pass on to these kids*" (a 12-year-old on a national team and a 10-year-old on the #1 National team in the country).

And of course: *I may have to break out some Cool Whip lids with the kids for hitting.*

TWENTY-THREE:
MICHAEL CUDDYER

David Wright appreciates Michael Cuddyer as the first player he saw who the scouts came to see. Michael Cuddyer was the first of Towny's guys to be drafted. "I call him the OG of the area," said David Wright. Pitcher John Curtice was selected after Michael Cuddyer in the First Round by the Boston Red Sox. "The scouts probably had no idea about Hampton Roads before he and his high school teammate John Curtice were drafted in the first round in 1996," explained David Wright.

David Wright as an 8th Grader, had a first-hand experience of being at the same high school the day that Cuddyer and Curtice were drafted in the 1996 MLB Draft.

“I spent half the day at Hickory Middle School taking classes, and then they would bus me to Great Bridge High School to take Spanish and Math. So, I was in the high school when they stopped school in the middle of the day, and it went over the loudspeaker to congratulate Michael and John Curtice at being drafted in the first round with the Major League draft,” said David Wright.

“I’ll never forget that day, I was in 8th grade, and I was like, I want this too. That’s when I set the goals to follow in those footsteps. I started to get to know Michael and be around him, work out with him and to use the same trainer as him,” said David Wright. “I would try to be in the gym with him as he was hitting, trying to emulate him and copy everything he did. That was the day where I first thought I wanted to be the next Michael Cuddyer from this area,” said David Wright.

Although Michael Cuddyer did not specifically remember David Wright as his shadow in the gym back in High School, he was sure David Wright would have seen the right things and a good example for him to emulate. Michael Cuddyer was always aware that someone would always be looking at him or to him to behave or model themselves. It could be David Wright, his family, friends, or someone he didn’t know yet. It was a responsibility he understood and never tried to hide from.

Integrity is doing the right thing, in the simplest terms, although no one is watching you or holding you accountable. Michael Cuddyer understands that it is a way of life for him but thinks everyone is a role model or can be someone’s hero, for the better or worse.

“I think we all have a responsibility to younger people to set examples. You’re going to be an influence regardless of whether you like it or not. Somebody is out there looking at you or looking up to you, whether you're a good person or a bad person somebody is looking up to you," said Michael Cuddyer. "It is your brother, your sister, a cousin, a nephew, or your next-door neighbor; you are somebody's role model. At a super young age, I understood that even before sports for me. So, I took a responsibility to do that," said Michael Cuddyer.

"When I got into pro ball, I really began to see David's passion for the game, and that's what kind of lured me to him. If anybody shows a desire for something, I'm willing to do whatever I can to help them," said Michael Cuddyer. "I wasn't around much when he was in school because I was playing nine months a year, but then once he got into pro ball, I tried to at least let him understand what minor League baseball is about. How to work out in the off-season, prepare, and get yourself ready. He didn't need much tutoring. So, he took it and went it," said Michael Cuddyer proudly.

Even as David Wright looked up to Michael Cuddyer, the roles were about to blur and reverse during the 2013 season. The All-Star game was scheduled for the Met's Citi Field, in essence, making the Met's David Wright the player-host for the All-Star Game and its festivities. The Home Run Derby is an event millions of fans tune in to watch as their favorite All-Stars launch baseball after baseball into the stands at a breathtaking distance and velocity.

Major League Baseball and its fans love to stack the teams with behemoth, monstrous players with enough flash and pizazz to stir the fans into a frenzy while punishing the baseball, wound especially tight for the event, into the bleachers.

As superstar players in New York, David Wright and Robinson Cano were designated as the respective league Captains. The American League was Cano, a future Met who would one day take

David Wright's locker at Citi Field. Prince Fielder of the Detroit Tigers, a huge and powerful man adept at prodigiously long home runs like his father, Cecil Fielder. Chris Davis, the Baltimore Orioles First Baseman who launched 53 home runs leading Major League Baseball that year, and Yoenis Cespedes of the Oakland Athletics, a future teammate on the 2015 Mets National League Champion team. The Home Run team Cano compiled was formidable and featured two players that became part of the four of the players who won the Derby twice.

David Wright took a different path; none of the players on his team previously won the Home Run Derby. Bryce Harper of the Nationals, Pittsburgh Pirate Pedro Álvarez and Michael Cuddyer of the Minnesota Twins.

On paper, it seemed like Michael Cuddyer did not have the same home run clout as the other well-known home run faces of Major League Baseball. But Cuddyer's face was one David Wright knew was one of the best guys and players in the league, and often undervalued and not afforded many chances on the National stage of baseball. David Wright, drawing from the lessons of respect, loyalty, and just doing the right thing as taught to him by people like his father, Coach Townsend, and Coach Erbe, knew it was the easy call to have Cuddyer on the team.

"I don't think David even understands how much that meant to me. He basically bucked Major League Baseball. They didn't want me in there since I wasn't a name, I wasn't a sexy contestant, and he stood up for me. It meant a lot; it was huge. I'm not going to say it was the reason why I joined the Mets, but he was a major reason why I went to the Mets. Everything was kind of a perfect storm with me going to the Mets, but that was a big factor," said Michael Cuddyer.

Michael Cuddyer certainly did not disappoint Major League Baseball fans or his Team Captain. Michael Cuddyer launched seven home runs in the first round. Cuddyer tied for first with 8 in the second round but fell one home run short in the combined two rounds behind Bryce Harper. Cespedes ended up clipping Harper in the Finals 9-8 to win the first of his two consecutive Home Run Derby titles. Cuddyer finished third, beating out the names fans knew as the swat monsters like Fielder and Davis. David Wright was near the bottom with a total of five home runs but was able to defend Citi Field against the Yankees and Robinson Cano, who finished with four.

He had all 5 tools, actually 4. His base running was just average. But I knew he had the tools to be a Big Leaguer. He was a good pitcher, 90 plus out of high school, could have pitched at the college level or beyond, but his hitting was special, said Gary Lavelle.

Michael Cuddyer was born in Norfolk, Virginia, on March 27, 1979. His parents were Henry Cuddyer and Marcia Harris. His father was a delivery truck driver, and his mother a bank officer. A 1997 Great Bridge High School graduate. Cuddyer was in the middle of a math test when the Twins selected him with the ninth pick in the 1997 draft. After being informed of the news by his principal, Cuddyer finished his test. Student Body President. In 1997, he was named to the All-America First Team by the American Baseball Coaches Association and Rawlings. In addition, Cuddyer was named Virginia's Player of the Year and Gatorade National Baseball Player of the Year in 1997. He was also a member of USA Today's All-Star and the USA Junior National teams in 1997. Twins signed him for a $1.85 million bonus and additional considerations for post-career college expenses. The

162 game average for 15-year MLB career is .277 with 21 home runs and 84 RBI.

- Only the third player, with John Olerud and Bob Watson, to hit for a Cycle for an American and National League team
- Played on the 1996 World Junior Championship Bronze Medal Team USA
- Played on the 1997 World Junior Championship Bronze Medal Team USA
- Minnesota Twins selected Cuddyer, 1st round (9th pick) of June MLB 1997 amateur draft
- An All-Star in both the American League and National League
- Two-time All-Star (2011 & 2013)
- NL Silver Slugger Award Winner (2013)
- NL Batting Average Leader (2013)
- 20-home run seasons: 4 (2006, 2009, 2011 & 2013)
- 30-home run seasons: 1 (2009)
- 100 RBI seasons: 1 (2006)
- 100 runs scored seasons: 1 (2006)

The Scouting Report by Baseball America before the 1997 MLB Draft

Drafted in the 1st round (9th overall) by the Minnesota Twins in 1997 (signed for $1,850,000).

Except for speed, Cuddyer has above-average tools across the board. He's slow out of the box but a good baserunner once he gets going. He has exceptional power and arm strength and has attracted a lot of interest as a pitcher. His work ethic has made him a favorite of scouts. He has become a quality high school shortstop through hard work, but third base still may be a better fit in pro ball.

In 2006, after a breakout season for the Twins, Cuddyer served as a substitute teacher at his old high school, Great Bridge High School. Earned the Twins nomination for the Roberto Clemente Award. Married Claudia Rente, a high school teacher, the same year.

In 2015, Cuddyer played with former Great Bridge High School alumni and fellow Towny Townsend student David Wright for the Mets and made it to the World Series.

Cuddyer hit .277 with 197 home runs and 794 RBI over his 15-year career playing for the Minnesota Twins, Colorado Rockies, and New York Mets.

Cool facts and quotes too good not to share.

- The New York Yankees were his favorite team growing up, and Don Mattingly was his favorite player. After several years already playing, he finally had the courage to ask Don Mattingly for his autograph.
- Michael Cuddyer is an outstanding amateur Magician.
- He would like to spend time today, if he could, with Towny Townsend: *If Towny were still around, I would just love to talk Baseball with him. I can talk Baseball all day long, and I think that's missing today, especially with our youth.*

- On the reasons for contract issues and troubling player–owner dynamics: *Major League Players are learning their history, with the Curt Floods, and that is why we are having what we are seeing now.*

TWENTY-FOUR:
PASSING THE TORCH

Chris Taylor is the face of the next generation of players from Hampton Roads to make a significant impact in Major League Baseball. Taylor followed in the footsteps of former Blaster and Driller, Mark Reynolds, and the Mr. Driller and Mr. National Ryan Zimmerman to the University of Virginia.

Chris Taylor was a 2012 Fifth Round pick by the Seattle Mariners. Taylor made his Major League debut in 2014 and played part-time until he was traded to the Los Angeles Dodgers during the 2016 season. Starting in 2017, Taylor has been a full-time player while playing the role of a Swiss army knife at 2B, 3B, S.S., and the outfield.

Driller Blue to Dodger Blue is paying off. Taylor has two 20 home run seasons, a National League Championship Most Valuable Player award in 2017, a World Series Championship in 2020, and made the 2021 All-Star team. After the 2021 season, Taylor signed a four-year/$60-million contract with a 2026 team option.

"I was a Driller from 8 until I was 16. A good portion of my childhood was spent playing in tournaments around the Country with the Drillers. It got me passionate about baseball, and I took it seriously. I know in Hampton Roads, it meant everything wearing Driller Blue. I was proud that everybody knew about the Drillers; it was definitely the team to be on when I was young," explained Chris Taylor.

Even years later, when Chris Taylor goes back to Hampton Roads, he sees the signs of what Coach Townsend, Coach Erbe, Coach Matt Sinnen, and Coach Gary Wright worked so hard to create. A baseball legacy.

"I know it's still carrying on. Whenever I go back, I always see a bunch of kids wearing travel ball and Driller hats. It's kind of become a staple of the area," explained Chris Taylor on the impact proudly displayed on the kids playing baseball now in Hampton Roads.

Chris Taylor knew the legacy of the Splendid 6 growing up in Hampton Roads. What may seem impossible to most kids, may have seemed possible since they all came up from the same fields and a lot of the same coaches and mentors.

"I was following all of their careers; I checked the score box for those guys every night to see how they played. Those are the guys looked up to growing up as a player," explained Chris Taylor.

For a player like Chris Taylor, seeing talent years ahead of him succeeding in high school, college, and then professional baseball was an onsite education and a shot of confidence to his baseball dreams.

As a youngster growing up, Chris Taylor would occasionally see the Splendid 6 in the flesh on the same high school fields he would soon dazzle as a player himself on, or maybe see some of the players at a Towny Townsend baseball clinic.

"I saw some of them play on their high school teams. I remember watching B.J. Upton play at Greenbrier Christian. I watched David Wright play against Princess Anne while he was playing for Hickory. I watched Ryan Zimmerman and Mark Reynolds play, too. Those were the guys I aspired to be like and follow in their footsteps," said Chris Taylor.

As a 10-year-old, short, and skinny player, Chris Taylor participated in one of the Towny Townsend baseball clinics hosted at Green Briar Christian Academy. The clinic had a special guest instructor: B. J. Upton, a player for Coach Towny Townsend and soon to be the #2 selection overall in the Major League Baseball draft. Coach Townsend could still make a strong impression on the kid, although he was fighting what would prove to be terminal cancer. Chris Taylor was just beginning his baseball path as Towny's own was being taken away

"I went to a baseball camp that B.J. Upton was helping with. I remember B.J. Upton throwing a ball from home plate and hitting the foul pole. I thought it was awesome. The camp had a great energy. Coach Towny Townsend was obviously extremely respected in the area. We were all excited to work with Coach Townsend," said Chris Taylor.

Chris Taylor was probably that little kid often seen on the side of high school games, tossing a ball or playing whiffle ball, trying to look and feel like the older kids and hoping one day to be just like them. Chris Taylor could quickly tell some of the Splendid 6 were on a baseball fast track and Chris Taylor reacted the same way many others would later behave in the presence of the Splendid 6.

The future All-Star player himself, one-day, would be giving autographs to adoring fans, but for a time he was just a star-struck kid hoping to get an autograph and a few words of conversation. The ballplayers were not only his baseball heroes, but they were also a roadmap of how to make the next levels of baseball he so badly wanted for himself.

"I knew David Wright was David Wright, and then the Upton brothers were a big deal up through high school. Zimmerman and Reynolds, more so when they went to the University of Virginia. I thought for sure they all would make it. But, of course, I may have had some hometown bias. I just knew these guys would be in the big leagues one day. I was just a little kid trying to get their autograph," said Chris Taylor.

Chris Taylor was able to get B.J. Upton's autograph at a high school game, Justin Upton's at high school games, Zimmerman, Cuddyer, Reynolds, and David Wright through various times in the area, either through friends or crossing Baseball paths.

Chris Taylor came from an athletic family, but it was not base-ball. Instead, Chris Taylor's father and grandfather went to Virginia Tech and wrestled for the college team. Although Chris Taylor split time among sports in season, baseball was his favorite, and his father would not stand in the way. In fact, he was Chris Taylor's earliest and favorite workout partner, coach, and mentor.

"My dad would print out these charts, they had like a thousand boxes, I would check off all the boxes; stuff like 100 swings, so I would do 100 swings off the tee. And then I'd marked off one of the rows and kept going on to the next box. I would do all that in the backyard into the net. We were also going to the field all the time. We would go to Great Neck recreational fields, and he would throw me round after round of batting practice. I think his labrum and shoulder are all messed up to this day. He probably needs arm surgery. He didn't just throw B.P. to me all the time as a teenager, but friends and teammates, too," explained Chris Taylor.

Most baseball and softball parents have buckets of balls in their garage from years of throwing and practicing the game with their children. Some parents brand the baseballs in hopes of getting them back on the field or hopefully over the fence, but mostly they go the way of the lost socks in a dryer. Almost like a time capsule and proof of what seems impossible can happen, if you are on a small baseball field in Hampton Roads, look down and you may still be able to find balls hit by a kid who later became an All-Star and World Series Champion. Three initials on the ball are a father and son baseball story.

"My dad always said we never bought a single baseball. I don't know how that worked, but eventually, we had like four buckets of baseballs in the garage. Every time at the field, there were always balls people would hit and leave behind. He would take those, bring them home, and write our initials, CAT, on them. To this day, there are probably some of those balls out there around the baseball fields in the area," said Chris Taylor.

Although Chris Taylor was from a line of wrestlers, he gravitated toward baseball before he could even remember.

"The whole family was wrestlers, but my father said I had a little whiffle ball bat, and I would take the bat in one hand and try to throw the whiffle ball in the air with the other and hit the ball, and that is when he decided he would be signing me up for T-Ball," said Chris Taylor.

But the Taylor household was not a pressure cooker for baseball. If he wanted to just focus on baseball, wrestling, soccer, or any combination of the three. He would just have to show personal initiative and drive, and his father would be there for him.

"I always loved baseball. I don't know if anybody instilled the love for the game in me like my dad did. I got my work ethic from him. He was always pushing me, just like I was pushing myself. He was definitely not holding me back, and he always wanted to go to the field with me. It was a mutual thing," said Chris Taylor.

By his own admission, Chris Taylor had to work hard and keep working to be where he is now as an MLB All-Star and World Series Champion. Chris Taylor was Tidewater Region Player of the Year and Virginia's 3-A Player of the Year in 2009, and somehow went undrafted in the 2009 MLB Draft. His freshman year at the University of Virginia, he was used sparingly before breaking out his sophomore year, starting all 68 games, and taking over at his favorite position, shortstop. Chris Taylor worked his way into the Fifth Round of the 2012 MLB Draft. Since then, his career is still climbing and even with a big MLB contract, but his work ethic does not ease up. Our conversations and interviews for this book were squeezed in as he was doing batting practice, drills, and workouts—Chris Taylor always working to be better and not wanting to ever ease up and fizzle out.

For Chris Taylor, he saw many kids like David Wright's old Blaster Teammate, Vince Sibal. Once bigger, faster, and stronger, kids who stopped growing or working as hard. The smaller and shorter kids who kept working and loved the game eventually catch up and can even leave the others by the wayside in baseball.

"There are a lot of guys who develop early and are superstars when they are nine and 10 years old. Then it is a game of catch-up to them in size and strength. They just kind of level off. It is like that at every level, even college," said Chris Taylor. "I played against guys in college that were superstars, and then five years later, I played against some in the minor leagues, and I was like, what happened to this guy? He used to be so much better than me. They didn't get better each and every year. That's the difference, guys that can constantly improve and get better, just even a little bit better, every year, those are the guys that that make it and have long careers rather than the guys that just sort of stay the same—they fizzle out," said Chris Taylor.

The catcher on a baseball team may be the manager on the field, but the shortstop is often the leader on the field. As coaches start from the lowest level of baseball to put the players into their positions, the shortstop is usually the best athlete. Each shortstop wants to play the position until it is their choice to move to another position or the choice is made for them.

Shortstops cling onto their position and know their competition on the baseball levels around them for it. Hall of Fame shortstop Phil Rizzuto of the New York Yankees kept a notebook to chronicle and write notes on all the shortstops on the Yankees Minor and Major League rosters to always try to outperform them.

In 1950, Rizzuto was particularly nervous about a power-hitting, switch-hitting shortstop tearing up the minor leagues. Mickey

Mantle was an 18-year-old shortstop playing for the Yankees Minor League club, the Joplin Miners. Mantle batted an incredible .383 and blasted 26 home runs for the Class C team. I have to repeat, as an 18-year-old. Mantle was not a polished player in the field, as he compiled 55 errors across 137 games. But Rizzuto was still nervous as he was seeing a future in baseball that might not include himself at shortstop for the Yankees much longer. Rizzuto really picked up his game that year, winning the Hickok Belt, awarded to the top professional athlete of the year, MVP for the American League and setting a record by handling 238 fielding chances at shortstop without an error.

Rizzuto was safe as the shortstop after 1951 Spring Training. The Yankees manager, Casey Stengel, saw too many errors first-hand and "banished" Mantle to center field to be tutored by Joe DiMaggio. Mantle became a Gold Glove outfielder later in his Hall of Fame career. Mantle also started a game in the Major Leagues at every position, but catcher and pitcher.

Hampton Roads now has a long history of players starting on their fields as a shortstop and making the Major Leagues. Michael Cuddyer, David Wright, Ryan Zimmerman, Mark Reynolds, B.J. Upton, Justin Upton, and Chris Taylor were shortstops in high school, college, or the Major Leagues.

For the kids in Hampton Roads, it was no different. Shortstop was where you wanted to see yourself and have others see you there. Just like Towny Townsend once did as a shortstop at Lake Taylor High School.

"From when I started the first time at shortstop and then in the Major Leagues, you have to battle your way into it each time. I'm sort of used to having a chip on my shoulder and being doubted.

It's something to be proud of. That's how I've gotten better, for sure. Growing up smaller made me have to work that much harder, and I always had a little bit of an ego," said Chris Taylor.

Chris Taylor was a late bloomer physically. He became used to scrapping and making himself be noticed on the field.

"I don't think I showed it openly and was not always proud of having the ego, but I always took a lot of pride and wanted to be the shortstop. I wanted to be the guy, so I had to fight for that a lot growing up. I played second base on most of the teams, but I always wanted to be the shortstop," said Chris Taylor.

But even the most elite baseball players must grudgingly respect and accept that someone else is the answer for the team at a certain position they wanted for themselves sometime. For Chris Taylor it happened with the Dodgers as Corey Seager, an NL Rookie of the Year, two-time All-Star, and two-time Silver Slugger, was entrenched at shortstop.

"I always thought I should be the shortstop, and that continued all the way through, even coming up with the Seattle Mariners from high school and UVA, and it was like that until I got to the Dodgers. They had Corey Seager, so I was like, Well, he is the shortstop. I had to find a new role for myself," said Chris Taylor.

Although the former Driller is younger than the Splendid 6, he has crossed the base baths with all of them, except for David Wright, on Major League fields. Chris Taylor introduced himself to Michael Cuddyer at second base during a Spring Training game, much like he would have approached him 20 years before as a kid in Hampton Roads—nervous, with big eyes, and lots of respect.

"I was playing shortstop, and he was on second base as a baserunner. I went up and introduced myself because I was just a Minor

Leaguer. I don't even know if he knew who I was, but I said something like, 'Hey Michael, I went to Cox High School.' He was super nice about it. I think he was stoked to see someone else from the area; it was only between pitches, but it was cool. The kid looking up to them is now looking at the Splendid 6, with all but one of them retired, as peers and the face of Hampton Roads in Major League baseball that Michael Cuddyer first started in 2001."

Over 20 years and counting of continuous representation from such a small sleepy section of Coastal Virginia.

"I would say I'm kind of in the same on the same level with all of them," said Chris Taylor. And as one of them now, Chris Taylor realizes and practices the Towny Townsend philosophies of "baseball people are the best kind of people," and "if you love baseball, you have to give it back."

The Splendid 6 and Chris Taylor are now in positions of public prominence and, in a sense, realize the importance of giving something back. Their coaches and parents growing up knew this and impressed it upon the players as they were coming up as people and players.

David Wright is one of the most charitable baseball stars, often behind the scenes, trying to blend in the best he can without cameras, just having compassion and helping as he can. David Wright established the David Wright Foundation in 2005 with the mission of increasing awareness about multiple sclerosis and raising money for various numerous sclerosis charities. David Wright also held a long-standing Annual Las Vegas Night to benefit Children Hospital of Kings Daughters. His work and acts helped raise millions of dollars for CHKD and other causes in Hampton Roads. Chris Taylor went to the events David Wright hosted for charity, and in time he formed his relationships to carry on the good works established by David Wright and the other ballplayers.

"I went to his events, I've seen everything he and those guys have done to give back, and it inspired me," explained Chris Taylor. 2022 is the first year Chris Taylor began to use California as his home base, but he still makes it back to Hampton Roads to do events and see family and friends. Even now, Chris Taylor lives only several miles from David Wright, but this time about five minutes from David Wright in California.

"This is my first year living in California. Previously I would go home for the winter and bounce back and forth to Los Angeles to work out with my hitting coaches. I went back for Thanksgiving this year (2021). I was there for a week and a half, and then I went back again in January for our CT3 charity event, "Driving for Hope" at Top Golf in Virginia Beach to benefit CHKD and the Roc Solid Foundation," said Chris Taylor.

Although he is mostly in California now, Chris Taylor keeps Hampton Roads in his heart. "I miss my family, I have a big family, and I miss my friends," said Chris Taylor. All my best friends are there, so you know I miss seeing them," explained Chris Taylor.

Chris Taylor began the CT3 Foundation to help raise money to help kids with cancer and to help the lives of all affected. Chris Taylor also raises donations and events for the Roc Solid Foundation and Children's Hospital of Kings Daughters. See info@ct3foundation.org.

TWENTY-FIVE: COOPERSTOWN

Induction at the Major League Baseball Hall of Fame in Cooperstown, New York, is a rare and valued honor for any ballplayer or contributor to the game of baseball. Players' and managers' contributions are on display with the all-time greats of the game for generations of baseball fans.

It is a huge accomplishment as a player to even be considered on the Hall of Fame ballot after retirement. The accomplishment of being on the ballot is often as far as it goes for most of the players regardless of accomplishments as a player. The writers make it harder with human factors such as biases, favoritism, grandstanding, hypocrisy, double-speaking, a lackadaisical approach, and even shock value Hall of Fame ballots for internet clicks or to help sell a story.

Even Derek Jeter, known as the model for the game on and off the field, was not above the voting shenanigans of the writers and deemed not worthy on an anonymous writer's ballot. As a result, it was the only ballot returned not naming Derek Jeter to the Hall of Fame. The single ballot was the only one withholding Jeter the honor of being the first unanimous selection for the Hall of Fame. The Yankees Mariano Rivera accomplished the first 100% vote a year later.

The parameters and how to vote are clear in the BBWAA Rules of Election in Section 4, Subsection 5 with just 23 words: "Voting shall be based upon the player's record, playing ability, integrity, sportsmanship, character, and contributions to the team(s) on which the player played."

Gambling and PEDs certainly fall under many players' integrity, sportsmanship, and character pitfalls. Ty Cobb was not a pleasant or tolerant person even by the standards of his day and is a monster under our present-day lens. But a heck of a player! He made it in easily.

The list of Hall of Fame players who allegedly violated the rules by using corked bats, too much pine tar, and sticky stuff on the ball is long and mostly laughed about and even celebrated in players like Mickey Mantle, like Gaylord Perry, or George Brett. But there is a darker, longer list with the bad deeds glossed over or simply brushed under the rug. The list of the players who committed crimes such as assault and battery, domestic violence, adultery, and even allegations of murder and rape is long, and a sad indictment of the rules and voting process in place.

Writers sometimes look past the very good players who are not friendly to the media to vote for players they like or who gave good interviews and access. Jeff Kent is an example of a very good player universally disliked by media and not enshrined in the Hall of Fame. But, on the other hand, a great player like Ted Williams could not be ignored, although he did not like the media, fans, and team ownership. Ted Williams hit a home run in what he knew would be his last career at-bat and would not even acknowledge the fans. I guess if a player does not like the media and the media does not like him, it is best to be as good as Ted Williams.

But some players cannot keep playing past a certain point to accrue those statistics on the back end of 30 years old. Hall of Fame eligibility is for players who played in at least parts of 10 Major League seasons, retired at least 5 years, and not on the Baseball ineligible list (a rule put in specifically to exclude possible write-in votes to induct players like Pete Rose or Shoeless "Joe" Jackson). But what of great players who, for some reason, can't produce those career trophy numbers?

Players like Clemens, Bonds, McGwire, and Sosa with no proven positive PED tests are kept out of the Hall, while David Ortiz became the first player to be voted in by the writers with a known positive MLB PED test. As a player, Pete Rose would be a first-ballot Hall of Famer, but because he admitted to gambling on his team to win as the manager is not. Baseball and gambling were an open secret before the 1919 Black Sox scandal. And 1905, 1912, 1914, and 1918 World Series were rumored to be influenced by game-fixers.

During a September 25th game in 1919, Tris Speaker, Dutch Leonard, Smokey "Joe" Wood, and Ty Cobb allegedly orchestrated a victory for Ty Cobb and the Tigers. Dutch Leonard was released by Ty Cobb in 1925 while Cobb was the player-manager. Leonard was not injured and at the time had an 11-3 Win-Loss record. No teams picked up Leonard, and he never played again.

Leonard decided to go to the American League Commissioner, Ban Johnson, in 1926 with the allegations of the fixed game in 1919, naming Speaker and Cobb and even producing letters between the four players seemingly admitting it in writing. The letters became public and caused an uproar. Cobb, Speaker, and Leonard were directed to testify at a hearing with the former judge and now Major League Baseball Commissioner Kennesaw Mountain Landis. Cobb denied the allegations, and Leonard declined to appear out of fear of a physical attack from Cobb. Speaker and Cobb were perhaps two of the best players of all-time up to that point, and Landis took no official action. But after the 1926 season, when both Tris Speaker and Ty Cobb were not retained as player-managers of their respective teams, it appeared as if the two had been unofficially banned from baseball. After threatening letters to Johnson and Landis from Cobb's lawyers and pressure from Cobb's connections in media, government, and industry, Cobb's baseball landscape softened up as he came back to play for the Philadelphia Athletics and Speaker found a spot with the Washington Senators. Speaker and Cobb are members of the Inaugural Hall of Fame Class of 1936. Leonard became a fruit farmer in California and had another chance to fight injustice.

In 1942 many Japanese Americans were forced into Internment Camps, with most losing their homes, property, and other holdings. Leonard stepped in and managed the farm of a Japanese family, promising it would be there for them once released. Once the family returned, Leonard kept his word. The land and profits were returned to the family. You can draw your own conclusion from that story about the credibility of the claims against Speaker and Cobb by Leonard.

The Major League's career Hits and Home Run Leaders are not in the Hall of Fame. So how does the actual "Cy Young" and his

511 pitching victories have to wait until his second year of eligibility? Eddie Matthews, a 3B with 512 home runs until his 5th year? Harmon Killebrew, with his 573 Home Runs until his 4th year of eligibility? David Ortiz, a DH with PED stain all over his Boston Red Sox jersey, is practically voted in with a ticker tape parade by the media. An incomplete and tarnished Baseball Hall of Fame is in Cooperstown.

A Baseball Hall of Fame without Yankees Catcher Thurman Munson is incomplete. Munson only played 11 Major League seasons before tragically dying in a plane crash at the young age of 32. Munson was an All-American at Kent State University before being drafted 4th overall in the 1968 draft by the New York Yankees. Munson earned the American League Rookie of the Year in 1970. Munson was selected to the All-Star Game in 1971, 1973-1978. Munson won three straight Gold Gloves from 1973 to 1975, earned the American League MVP, and became the Yankees Captain in 1976, the first since Lou Gehrig.

Munson is perhaps the best postseason catcher in history, hitting .357 with 3 home runs and 22 RBI. He also threw out 24 runners. Munson played in six postseason series totaling only 30 games. Munson, as Team Captain, took the N.Y. Yankees to three straight World Series in 1976–1978, with the Yankees losing the first one against the Big Red Machine of the Cincinnati Reds and then winning the next two against a former fellow New York Team, the Los Angeles Dodgers. Munson's Wins above Replacement (WAR) is 46.1.

As a comparison, Ted Simmons is a Hall of Famer. He was inducted into the Hall of Fame in 2020 by the Veteran's Committee. Simmons was a fine catcher across his 21 seasons with a WAR of 50.3. Both played in the same baseball era; Simmons was drafted out of high school as 10th pick overall in the 1967 MLB Draft, with his rookie eligibility expiring in 1970. In 1994, Simmons, in his first and only year of Hall of Fame voting eligibility, received 3.7% of votes from the BBWAA. Simmons was subsequently dropped from further consideration by the voting members of the BBWAA for failing to hit the threshold of at least 5%. During his first year of eligibility, Munson hit 15.5% and stayed on the ballot for the maximum allowed at the time of 15 years with not once falling below the 5% threshold.

In 1994 Munson and Simmons squared off against each other in the BBWWA vote. Munson was able to hit 6.8% on his 14th year of candidacy. Simmons hit 3.7%. Munson and Simmons squared off again in 2019 in the revamped Veteran's Committee Vote. The 16-person committee is composed of a blend of former players, executives, and baseball historians. Ted Simmons earned 13 of the 16 votes and his induction. Thurman Munson was at three or lower votes from the committee. Ted Simmons is the only player to be dropped for not getting past the first-year ballot threshold and still making it to the Hall of Fame as a player. What changed with these two players over 15 years between 1994 and 2019? Simmons and his cumulative statistics became more appreciated in the new age of baseball's advanced statistics. Munson's statistics stopped with his death at an Ohio airfield.

Simmons was a National League All-Star six times in the 1970s. Munson had seven All-Star Games in the 1970s. Johnny Bench and Simmons were the NL best catchers and the AL had the best in Munson and Carlton Fisk. Bench, Fisk, and Simmons are in the Hall of Fame. Try and find a scout or manager that saw Simmons as the better of the two in the 1970s. It wouldn't happen.

Did Simmons somehow get better over the years and add to his statistics to become a slam dunk over Munson as a player? Or is the Hall of Fame a system backed on subjective opinions and factional dealing and maneuvering at times?

It probably is simply, and more innocently, that baseball is a game of milestones. Five-hundred home runs, 3,000 hits, and 300 wins are numbers that, without suspected PEDs or other off-field issues, ensure eventual induction to Cooperstown. Except for David Ortiz.

David Arias signed with the Seattle Mariners in 1992 just after turning 17. It may have been a Julio Franco-birthday style celebration as questions of his actual age have dogged Ortiz for years; sometimes he is older and sometimes younger. After four years in the Mariners farm system, Ortiz was a player to be named later in a trade with the Minnesota Twins. With the trade complete he asked to be called by his preferred name of David Ortiz. Six years with the Twins resulted in 58 home runs before the Twins released him after the 2002 season. Ortiz had his spot replaced on the roster by Jose Morban, a player who never played a game for the Twins and in his one year of MLB with the 2003 Baltimore Orioles finished with two home runs batting .141.

The 2003 season for David Ortiz had him reportedly testing positive for PEDs, hitting 31 home runs, 101 RBI and batting .288 while placing fifth in the American League MVP Award as voted on by the Baseball Writers Association of America. (BBWAA) The same voters vote each year for the National Baseball Hall of Fame.

Bonds, Clemens, and Ortiz all reportedly tested positive in 2003 by MLB for PEDs. Like Clemens and Bonds, Ortiz did not appear to fail an MLB test since then. Clemens and Bonds are both left out of the Hall of Fame by the voters while Ortiz is in.

David Ortiz is given pass after pass from the media and MLB. Incidents and worrisome items occurred, like being shot and almost killed after a drug dealer placed a hit on him to be carried out by the police. The Dominican Republic's Police and Government actions and investigations into the shooting were incompetent and untruthful, at best. David Ortiz had a restraining order placed on him by his former partner, the mother of his son for alleged domestic violence, threatening and intimidating actions.

In 2011, David Ortiz won the Roberto Clemente Award, given annually to the MLB player who best exemplifies the game of baseball, sportsmanship, community involvement, and the individual's contribution to his team. To be fair, baseball awarded Pete Rose in 1976, Sammy Sosa in 1998, and Curt Schilling in 2001. Not one of the Splendid 6 won the Roberto Clemente award, and I, for one, believe it demonstrates a failure by MLB.

Only in Boston did one street name get taken down from a now-deceased team owner, Tom Yawkey, enshrined in the National Baseball Hall of Fame, with a troubling past to a player with a troubling past. Don't forget to take David Ortiz Drive straight to the "Big Papi" David Ortiz Bridge.

I bought the question of Ortiz to Michael Cuddyer if Ortiz deserves to be in the Hall of Fame. "Seventy-five percent is a lot of people to get to vote for you, and Ortiz at the end of the day got it. If you can get 75% of a community to vote for anything, to vote for you, you've done something. Yeah, it is what it is," said Michael Cuddyer. On seeing the whole of the question posed, I rephrased the question and asked Michael Cuddyer the more direct question: as a former MLB Player, an All-Star, and an Ortiz teammate with the Minnesota Twins, did he deserve to be in the Hall of Fame? "That was not the question you first asked," smiled Michael Cuddyer.

Ted Simmons did not hit any of those crown jewel milestones, but he achieved longevity and played for 21 years. Simmons played a little more than 1,000 games compared to Munson. Simmons compiled numbers padding his stat line through the 1988 season and Munson died during the 1979 baseball season. Simmons started 100 games or more at catcher during a season 9 out of 10 years for the 1970s. The 1980's were not as dominant for Simmons as he was only able to catch 100 or more games during 2 of the 9 years he played in the 1980s. From 1983 to 1988, he spent more time on the field in other positions than catcher.

Catchers 30 years older and above get old and slow fast. Even the great Johnny Bench couldn't hit 30 home runs or knock in 100 runs after 29, spending his last few seasons at first and third base. Yogi Berra spent his last few years for the Yankees before playing for the Mets in their outfield. Munson started to slow down in his age 31 and 32 seasons, but still managed to hit .297 and .288 during nearly 1,000 at-bats. Munson had his life taken too young and probably the chance to be placed among the all-time greats at Cooperstown.

Munson may not be the best example of a New York baseball Captain who may not receive enough Hall of Fame support for enshrinement because their career is curtailed and not able to compile lengthy milestone stats.

Willie Randolph? Ron Guidry or Don Mattingly? Yes, all have Cooperstown valid arguments for enshrinement, but there was another, David Wright.

David Wright was on a Hall of Fame trajectory to become an all-time great third baseman like Mike Schmidt, Eddie Matthews, or George Brett. Keep in mind only Mike Schmidt played his position at third base deep into his 30s. Mike Schmidt played it right up until the day he felt he couldn't play it anymore and promptly announced his retirement mid-road trip on May 29, 1989. Schmidt never played again, but put his uniform one more time that year at MLB fans' request. Schmidt, although retired, was voted as the starting 3B for the National League 1989 All-Star team. Schmidt tipped his hat while he was in uniform and did not play as Howard Johnson of the Mets replaced Schmidt's spot as the starter.

George Brett played until he was 33 at third base, and the next seven years were primarily spent at first base and designated hitter with only 15 games at third base. Eddie Matthews was done at third base at 34 years old, playing his next three seasons at first base. David Wright hurt his back right at the peak of what should have been his peak years as a third baseman.

In 2011, Wright was coming off five straight All-Star seasons with five of his seven seasons to date with 100 RBIs. Five of those seasons were also at hitting .300 or better. An All-Star Captain playing in New York with numbers like that has a clear path to Cooperstown. Then at 28 years old, during the 2011 season, he hurt his back, and his career changed. The Hall of Fame path may have been made more difficult a couple years earlier, though.

Matt Cain beaned David Wright in the helmet in August of 2009; some fans believe that Wright's batting aggressiveness changed, ever so slightly, making the outside corner even more inviting for a pitcher. Did Wright have injuries hampering him, like former Yankees Captain Don Mattingly? Or was it more like a young 1960s prodigy playing for the Boston Red Sox?

The story of Tony Conigliaro is one of the saddest in baseball history. Conigliaro was only a teenager when he first played for the Red Sox. In 1964, at only 19 years old, Conigliaro stroked 24 home runs and led the American League the following year with 32 home runs. He was the youngest American League player to reach 100 career home runs. Conigliaro's career started out white-hot and Cooperstown-bound.

Conigliaro was a tough player and not willing to give anything up around the plate. Pitchers of the 1960s and 1970s were tough too, and certainly would attempt to keep the batter off the plate with an inside fastball. Pitchers now must navigate baseballs around what looks like a linebacker wearing hockey goalie gear guarding the strike zone. Different times and another game.

Conigliaro had a habit of crowding the plate, never giving in an inch. Blazing fastballs up and in were thrown and Conigliaro just would move his head and settle into the next pitch. Ted Williams, some say the greatest hitting tactician of all-time, Towny's favorite player and the reason Townsend wore his beloved #9, was scared for Conigliaro.

The Dog Days of August 1967 saw the Boston Red Sox deep into the Pennant Chase. Ted Williams urged a friend of Conigliaro's to pass the message to him before his next game on August 18th that he was crowding the plate too much and the pitchers would start to throw at him. The Red Sox couldn't afford to lose him.

The message was relayed to Conigliaro before the game on August 18th. But Conigliaro was in a slump and planned to dig in even closer. Against the California Angels, Jack Hamilton came inside with a fastball barreling Conigliaro into the left eye and cheek-bone. His helmet was of no value as he moved his head so fast before impact that the helmet came flying off. Although the damage was done, he never lost consciousness. The Red Sox managed to make the playoffs that year, but never would have been in the position to make the playoffs without his contributions well into August. But without him, they were less of a team and ultimately lost in the World Series without him.

Conigliaro's vision was so compromised that his doctor told him it would not be safe for him to play anymore. If Conigliaro looked straight at the pitcher, he could not see the ball, so he began to look just left of the pitcher and trained himself to track the ball using just his peripheral vision. Perhaps to keep playing, he also tried to pitch in the 1968 season. Conigliaro was unsuccessful in going 0-3 with 15 runs given up in the minors before a sore arm shut him down.

The 1969 and 1970 seasons, with Conigliaro still relying on eyesight that couldn't even see the pitcher directly or the ball in the pitcher's hand, he willed himself to 20 home runs and 83 RBI to take the 1969 Comeback Player of the Year Award. And 1970 was even more impressive as he was able to slug 36 home runs and drive in 116 RBI.

The Red Sox traded Conigliaro after his big 1970 year while his value was high. Which team deals a player who by age 25 slugs 160 home runs and coming off a career-high 36 home run and 116 RBI season? The Red Sox did like him as a player, but they probably knew Conigliaro had somehow made magic in 1969 and 1970 and would not have many more rabbits to pull out of his hat in the future. Nearing the All-Star break with the California Angels in 1971, he was hitting .222 with 4 home runs and 15 RBI. After a game on July 9th, Conigliaro decided it was time to retire due to his headaches from eye strain and his vision loss.

Conigliaro still had more left in his baseball tank. He wanted to play again a few years after initially retiring. Conigliaro paid his own way to Boston Red Sox 1975 Spring Training and against the odds, earned a spot in their Opening Day lineup as the designated hitter. Opening Day saw him with his first at-bat, have a hit, receive a three-minute Standing Ovation, and cap that off by pulling starting a double-steal to bring future Hall of Famer, Carl Yastrzemski in for a run. The next day he bashed a home run against 20-game winner Mike Cuellar.

The early success did not keep up, and he was outrighted in June to their Triple-A team, the Pawtucket Red Sox, and shortly after decided to retire, this time a lasting one. But as ex-players tend to do, he stayed around the game, first as a broadcaster in Providence and then San Francisco. In 1982, Conigliaro was seemingly back on his way to the Red Sox, this time as the color commentator for the Boston Red Sox games. Sadly, like his playing career, it wouldn't happen as planned. A career that started out with cruise control to Cooperstown ended slowly and finally to an end after eight years. His return as Red Sox color commentator never happened.

On January 9, 1982, he suffered a heart attack on the way to an airport. Conigliaro suffered irreversible brain damage and was hospitalized for two months before being discharged to the care of his family. Conigliaro died eight years later, in 1990. Nearly 60 years after Tony Conigliaro came up for the Red Sox, he still holds a special place to the fans of the Boston Red Sox.

Like Tony Conigliaro, David Wright learned to battle through his challenges and injuries. The character and loyalty David Wright showed the Mets was returned to David Wright by the franchise. The following six seasons, David Wright grinded to make two NL All-Star teams but could not get to the 100 RBI milestone he was used to getting to and "only" hit .300 twice. Surgery after surgery just bought more and more rehab and cast his career further in doubt as the only statistic he was able to compile was games not played.

Many players of his caliber and track record may have switched to a more manageable position on the body other than third base. Position changes to save the body wear and tear to prolong a career is often done and may have helped David Wright to Cooperstown. Ultimately, David Wright retired when he knew his body and mind could not perform to a level close enough to what he, the Mets, and their fans had come to expect.

David Wright has a Win above Replacement-162 game average of 5.0. The top 15 Hall of Fame third baseman standard is at 5.1 WAR/162. David Wright is right there. Mike Schmidt is far away the highest at 7.2. Schmidt is debatably the best of all-time at third base. The only others at 6.0 and above are Eddie Matthews and Wade Boggs. Players like Edgar Martinez are listed as third baseman with their stats but skew the numbers because just a small fraction of the games played at third base for the career. David Wright's 39.5 seven-year peak WAR is just below the average 3B Hall of Famer of 15-member average of 43.0. David Wright only started two games in the field other than 3B, which was as the more difficult shortstop. Wright also started three games at D.H.

David Wright will probably never make the Hall of Fame. A record of 242 home runs is well short of 500, and 1,777 hits are well short of 3,000. It is tantalizing to think, "What if?" David moved positions to protect the wear and tear on his body and back a little more. What stats could he have compiled during those eight compromised seasons and the five more he could squeeze out of his body to age 40 like George Brett was able to do? Five-hundred home runs and 3,000 hits are certainly realistic opportunities.

The 162-game average for David Wright is Hall of Fame-worthy, hitting .296 with 26 home runs and 99 RBI. For comparison, George Brett, with years away from 3B, hitting .305 with 19 home runs and 96 RBI. Eddie Matthews hitting .271, 35 home runs, and 98 RBIs. Wright hangs with them both. I won't compare Mike Schmidt because he is Mike Schmidt., but if I did, it would be .267, 37 home runs, and 107 RBI. But that is Mike Schmidt.

The bottom line is if the BBWAA Rules of Election in Section 4, Subsection 5 is applied in the matter as intended under the rules: "Voting shall be based upon the player's record, playing ability, integrity, sportsmanship, character, and contributions to the team(s) on which the player played." David Wright and perhaps some of the other Splendid 6, like those that have shown such outstanding qualities stated in the election rules, that the Minnesota Twins placed Michael Cuddyer into their Hall of Fame, and it is a near certainty that both David Wright and Ryan Zimmerman will be by their teams as well. Nobody would be surprised if the Statue of Wright or Zimmerman is placed at the respective franchise stadium or Spring Training facilities. These players breeze past five of the six tenets of the BBWAA Vote of Ability, Integrity, Sportsmanship, Character, and Contribution to the teams played on by the player. The long-term statistics of many Hall-of-Famers are often padded on the back ends of careers, often as a below-average replacement player keeping players like David Wright, Michael Cuddyer, Ryan Zimmerman, Thurman Munson, Fred Lynn, Willie Randolph, Ron Guidry, and Don Mattingly from the Hall of Fame.

Do coaches like Towny Townsend deserve a place alongside baseball greats in Cooperstown? Yes and no. Here is why and how it could happen in some way.

Towny Townsend hit .200 with 0 home runs and 32 runs batted in across two seasons is "A" Ball in the Carolina League's Winston-Salem team during 1974 and 1975. Unfortunately, his numbers in the Minor Leagues will not get him there. But the qualities he possessed and helped pass down to hundreds, if not thousands of kids and ballplayers resonated through a region of the country first and then opened the eyes of millions of baseball fans worldwide. A man of integrity, character, loyalty, and sportsmanship, Towny picked the kids and players who would perform well with proper coaching. Still, he chose the parents and players upon the potential to be even more and give back.

The Buck O'Neil Lifetime Achievement Award is presented by the Hall of Fame's Board of Directors not more than once every three years to honor an individual whose extraordinary efforts enhanced baseball's positive impact on society, broadened the game's appeal, and whose character, integrity and dignity are comparable to the qualities exhibited by O'Neil.

The award, named after the late Buck O'Neil, was first given in 2008, with O'Neil being the first recipient. The honor was announced as if you could easily place the name Towny Townsend there as well as Buck O'Neil's.

"The Board of Directors of the National Baseball Hall of Fame and Museum is thrilled to honor Buck O'Neil as the first recipient of this award, named after him," said Jane Forbes Clark, chairman of the National Baseball Hall of Fame and Museum. "Buck touched every facet of baseball, and his impact was among the greatest the game has ever known. The Board recognizes this impact Buck had on millions of people, as he used baseball to teach lessons of life, love, and respect. His contributions to the game go well beyond the playing field. This Award will recognize future recipients who display the spirit Buck showed every day of his life.

A Buck O'Neil Lifetime Achievement Award would appear something like this for Towny Townsend: The 2023 Recipient of the

Buck O'Neil Lifetime Achievement Award was Marvin "Towny" Townsend. Towny Townsend often said, "Baseball people are the best kind of people." Townsend collected baseball people and was inspired by them and inspired them.

Townsend's service to baseball and people spanned four decades as a Minor League player, coaching baseball at youth, high school, and college levels. Townsend was the driving force to ensure baseball competition and the coaching to help propel and prepare dozens of players to professional baseball careers and dozens more to college scholarships. In addition, the creation of his AAU travel organization, the Blasters, and helping to inspire a rival Drillers program, made MLB history with a concentration of talent developed at a hyper-local community level for Major League Baseball. Those players include some of the best players in the early 2000s through today.

Townsend's own professional baseball career was cut short after he and his mother were verbally assaulted by racial epithets from his own baseball team. At the time, she sat in the stands watching her son during a game. Townsend was compelled to act and protect his mother from the escalating dangers of verbal onslaught. Towny Townsend broke the jaw of his own Red Sox Minor League manager during the escalating racial incident. After only a season and a half, the Boston Red Sox released the four-time Major League draft pick.

Towny never played professional baseball again.

Towny Townsend's expansive reach is displayed with his coaching and mentoring of thousands of players in the Hampton Roads area of Virginia, turning the previous sleepy baseball fields into hotbeds attracting every Major League team scouting the area and helping players like Michael Cuddyer, David Wright, Ryan Zimmerman, B.J. Upton, and Justin Upton being First Round picks and starring in the Major Leagues from 2001 through today. Although Mark Reynolds was not a First Rounder, he was a 40 Home Run Player for the Arizona Diamondbacks and retired with nearly 300 home runs.

Towny Townsend also returned to his former high school and became a role model as a person and a baseball mentor and head coach at a predominantly African American school, previously not producing a consistent baseball team into a championship-caliber team. In addition, Townsend worked tirelessly while personally battling and ultimately losing a battle with cancer for MLB Baseball's RBI Program to help promote and provide equality in baseball.

Towny Townsend passed away in 2007 after a nearly seven-year battle with cancer.

TWENTY-SIX:

BABE RUTH—BASEBALL HERO AND CANCER PIONEER

Babe Ruth was a man of excess during a time we often fondly look back at in baseball history. The good old days before the shift, closers, designated hitters, pitch-counts, and steroids. But since then, we have improvements shaping Major League Baseball such as integration, night baseball, all MLB games available on TV, and educated players on health and lifestyle. Babe Ruth and his diet, training, and lifestyle would have been scandalous today, but it worked for him and his playing career, yet ultimately probably did not translate to a long and healthy life after retiring from the Boston Braves in 1935. Babe Ruth and his baseball career could pale compared to what he did for us later. Babe Ruth played a part in saving what will turn out to be millions of people from cancer. Wait, what?

Babe Ruth lived as large as the numbers he put down. Ruth held the record for most home runs (714), had a batting average of .342, batted in 2,213 runs, had a slugging percentage of .690, got on base 47.4 percent of the time he batted, scored 2,174 runs, hit for 5,793 total bases, and was walked 2,062 times. And of course, he set the record for home runs in a single season with 60, which has now been topped several times.

Ruth's numbers are without the benefit of any steroids or other traditional performance enhancement drugs. But Babe Ruth was a prodigious drinker and smoker. Deliveries of at least one case of whiskey were delivered to his room for each series on the road, and his bathtub was filled with bottles of beer. All this even during the dry days of Prohibition. His appetite for booze and tobacco was as deep as his home runs blasted into the stands.

Sometimes, when I reflect on all the beer I drink, I feel ashamed. Then I look into the glass and think about the workers in the brewery and all of their hopes and dreams. If I didn't drink this beer, they might be out of work, and their dreams would be shattered. I think, "It is better to drink this beer and let their dreams come true than be selfish and worry about my liver, explained Babe Ruth on his drinking.

In the fall of 1946, Babe Ruth began to feel sick, his voice hoarse and pain behind his left eye. Medical care and science were not as advanced as they are now, and the doctors thought it was sinus infection or bothersome teeth. Several of his back teeth were pulled out by a dentist to alleviate pain. It did not work. Ultimately it was revealed Babe Ruth had cancer of the neck, throat, and nasopharynx. Surgery was done, and follow-up radiation treatments did little except Babe Ruth losing his hair, becoming depressed, and losing 100 pounds.

Babe Ruth never knew he had cancer. However, he probably understood on some level as his hospital was a traditional cancer treatment hospital, Memorial Hospital, now known as Memorial-Sloan Kettering.

His doctors were frantically scrambling to find a cure for the cancer that would eventually kill the baseball star who rewrote the game. Mustard Gas killed thousands of soldiers during World War I. Many of the soldiers inhaling the chemical weapon lived to come home to only die young from the long-term effects of the chemical inhalation. The weapon was designed to kill, and it killed men like a Hall-of-Famer pitcher winning 373 games, Christy Matthewson. But Ruth received the same poisons, now harnessed as a weapon to kill cancer cells in humans. Nitrogen mustard, called teropterin, was administered daily for six weeks. The trial-and-error treatment for Babe Ruth made him perhaps the first cancer patient to receive sequential radiation and chemotherapy. The "Babe Ruth" treatment is now the so-called "chemo-beamo" standard treatment for cancer. Methotrexate, a chemical similar to teropterin, is still used to treat cancer and autoimmune diseases.

As Ruth explained in his 1948 autobiography, "I realized that if anything was learned about that type of treatment, whether good or bad, it would be of use in the future to the medical profession and maybe to a lot of people with my same trouble."

Babe Ruth quickly felt relief as neck lymph nodes began reducing, gaining close to 80 pounds he previously lost and his overall pain lessening. The respite gave him an extra six months or so of life, allowing him to see the movie of his life for the New York premiere of "The Babe Ruth Story" and presenting Yale University a manuscript for his autobiography, "The Babe Ruth Story" to their Baseball Captain at Yale University, a first baseman named George Bush. Ruth also attended an event at Yankee Stadium honoring the 25th Anniversary of Yankee Stadium. Though a shadow of the man Yankee fans remembered as blasting the first home run at "the House the Ruth Built," Ruth carried on and tried to give fans another moment with him.

Babe Ruth used the precious last of his life as a sprint to please others, showing up at events and doing what he could to make people happy. Babe Ruth took visitors and answered letters right to the very end. The last thing he did while still conscious before dying was to autograph his book for one of his nurses. Babe Ruth died in 1948 and was only 53.

TWENTY-SEVEN:
TOWNY AND A LONG GOODBYE

Like Babe Ruth, Towny Townsend had cancer, but he knew it and wanted people to know he was fighting it and planning to beat it.

Towny went to a local high school internet baseball board that almost reads like a blog now. Towny shared his battles, keeping a positive attitude and trying to build others right up to near the day of his death. Below are some examples of what he wrote during his days battling cancer. They are not edited, as I wanted to directly voice Towny's words.

I know that there will be a number of stories told in the coming days regarding the coaching career of one of the great high school coaches to ever grace our area. I would like to tell those who read these pages about a story that reaches beyond the baseball field and shows the inner man. In 2001 after my personal battle with cancer, G.C.A. played First Colonial in the Beach Bash. Upon completion of the game Norbie and his F.C. parents and kids humbled me and my family with a significant cash contribution to the "Friends of Towny Townsend fund" that helped my family handle mounting medical expenses. He donated the entire proceeds from gate receipts and concessions to my family after a tough loss. We talked at great length about the things that truly matter without ever discussing the game. He showed true compassion, understanding, and a sense of humanity that will be sorely missed at F.C. and impossible to replace. Coaches are often misunderstood, second guessed, and ridiculed but Norbie's career stands on its own merit and has no peer in Tidewater. First Colonial will have an easier time finding a good baseball coach than they will be finding a man of character who knows Baseball. Good luck my friend.

5/25/04 8:06 a.m.

The Virginia Blasters 12-U finished 2nd in Cooperstown, N.Y., losing to the Missouri Orioles 7-2. The blasters finished the 80-team tournament at 10-1. I am very proud of these 12-year-old young men who represented our state by not only playing excellent Baseball but showed tremendous character and heart. I would also like to use this thread to thank the hundreds of members from around the country as well as here at home who have sent me extremely positive and motivational messages regarding my battle with throat cancer and my impending surgery this Thursday. I thank all of you from my family and the very depth of my soul. Taking 13 young boys to Cooperstown this past week was the perfect pre-operation activity for an old coach like me. My boys just kept charging my battery and fought every inning to the last out. I plan on taking their spirit and

God's grace to the surgeon's table. Thanks again to one and all; I have been humbled by your words of love and encouragement.

– Towny Townsend

7/17/05 8:02 a.m.

Well...I am out of the hospital and recuperating at home. Working on the speaking skills so I'll be ready come spring! I read the website regularly and I've been humbled by the prayers and good wishes. I won't be able to talk to anyone for a while, so feel free to email me. It helps with my therapy. Ha ha. Thanks to everyone and I'll see you soon.

– Towny

8/7/05 9:07 p.m.

Thanks, Cleveland Dad and all that have posted on this web page. Over the last month I have heard from baseball people all over the country. My surgery lasted 14 hours and then I went in the next day for a six-hour surgery when I developed a blood clot. I was unconscious for 12 days and remember nothing from that time. After a 15-day stay in the hospital, I was released 2 weeks ago. All of our prayers are being answered. They did not take my voice box, so with speech therapy I will speak again. I am unable to swallow and am being fed thru a G-tube, but I feel blessed and believe that I will learn to swallow again. I was raised that Baseball was more than a game when you teach life lesson's through it. I am grateful that I had a father and coaches that looked at the hard times in the game as opportunities to make me stronger. I am also thankful for family, posters, and friends who have acted like teammates and picked me up when I couldn't get the job done myself. I'm reminded of a saying "that life, like baseball, must be coached." I could not have imagined going through this life experience without my baseball life lessons. Cancer was the most difficult competition that I ever faced but like all opponents it brought out the best in me and others. Cleveland Dad you hit the nail on the head...Every day is a blessing now. You obviously know how I feel, have felt that way yourself, and we share a very similar result. Thanks again to all and I will gladly keep you up to date as I come all the way back.

– Towny

8/22/05 4:22 p.m.

Dear "Friends of Towny Townsend," I would like to take this opportunity to thank the baseball family near and far for the daily support emotionally, physically, and financially that has been a constant since my operation in July. Cancer is the most difficult opponent I have ever faced but I have not had to do it alone. God's hands were on me and he assembled an incredible team to aid me and my family in going on the offensive. A special thanks to Ron Smith (Blaster) Ron's father was Billy Smith...who pitched in the bigs for Phillies and Cardinals and died from the same cancer of the throat that afflicted me. James Cotterell, Tim Miller, and Glenn Miller who worked tirelessly on my foundation's behalf. I would also like to thank the myriad of posters from all over the country and friends, players, coaches, etc. too numerous to mention here for your constant prayers, encouragement, and thoughts. Know that although I was hit a bad hop, we have knocked it down in front, are picking it up bare-handed, and are set to make the throw. God bless each and every one of you this holiday season!!! Give thanks daily...that's what I'll be doing.

– Towny

11/22/05 3:11 p.m.

Thanks, Guys, for your kind words and support. Please forgive me if this Post is a little rambling but I'm really overwhelmed by the opinions expressed on this message board. It's hard to believe that just 7 months to the day I was in Norfolk General Hospital unconscious after 2 days of surgery. I remained unconscious for another 14 days before awaking to see my wife in front of me with both thumbs up. We had pre-arranged that if I awoke that the left thumb meant that my voice box had not been removed and the right meant that my mother who also was dying of cancer was still alive. I was fortunate to be with her when she passed even though I was incapable of speaking to her. In spite of these circumstances and with the help of so many baseball people I felt like the most blessed man on the face of the earth. Cancer does not define me, but it helped motivate me to do some things that I probably never would have done without it. I got together with some boys that played for me and that I have known since they were little boys on the back fields of Chesapeake... David Wright (Mets), Mike Cuddyer (Twins), Matt Smith (Rangers) and we have just completed a DVD on hitting and an invention that I've patented called the Towny Townsend hitting disc. Some of you have seen me use them over the years with my teams, camps, and lessons. The neat thing is a portion of proceeds will go to two worthy causes: the David Wright Foundation to battle MS and the American Cancer Society's Relay for Life to honor my mother and to whip cancer in my lifetime. I also am finishing up a book called *Dad, Let's Play Catch*. Without giving too much away it's about coaching your own children. I draw on personal experiences to make it informative and I hope funny. I did this to honor my father who is with my mother now and also to benefit cancer research. The DVD should be out in April and the book this summer. I have been the kick-off speaker for Relay for Life in Norfolk and Virginia Beach and have joined the ACS locally in helping great people from all walks of life get after cancer. So, guys, life is so much like Baseball, it's not a question if your life/game will ever hit bottom. It will...the question is how high and quick you'll bounce once you do that counts. Trust me when I say that all that everyone has done for me and my family with God's grace made lifting myself out of the dirt one of the most rewarding experiences of my life. Thank you, Gary Spedden (Ocean Lakes), with your desire to support the friends of Towny Townsend... money raised on my behalf has not just gone to my bills and therapy but also has benefited the Sidney Oman Cancer Treatment Center, the American Cancer Society, and families that have cancer in their lives. I have said it many times..."Baseball people are just the best people." Every one of you validates that to me every day. "I have survived to laugh at the odds and to live my life so well that death will tremble to take me." God bless you all.

3/23/06 7:17 p.m.

It is true my cancer has returned and is in both lungs...Cathy and I just found out yesterday and we told Sean and Chase last night, so things are still up in the air as to prognosis, but I see Dr. Sinesi at Sidney Oman Cancer Treatment Center tomorrow and then oncologist on the 23rd...My guess is chemo and radiation, but I'll know more later. Redbird5, did you ever think that when you were a young boy, and I was hitting groundballs to you in the back fields of Great Bridge, that someday this old coach would be thanking you for praying for him? Reminds me of that old John Lennon song quote, "Life is what happens when you're making other plans." Cleveland Dad, I'm getting my game face on today thanks for your prayers...I'll get after this thing again I promise.

5/16/06 8:24 p.m.

The Metheny family, I am honored and humble to receive an award that is named for your father. He was a mentor to me and a role model. My fondest memory of him may surprise you but it was not on a baseball field but on a creek in creeds fishing for Brim and Perch with cane poles. Your dad loved to fish and talk ball and I learned more about him and the family he cherished that day. Your dad had this little twinkle in his eyes when he spoke of you that was Santa Claus like. It's awesome to be recognized as the 30th recipient of the award. The list of past winners is a staggering array of baseball people from Tidewater. When I was young, I was very hot headed as many who read these pages would attest and it was your father and David Rosenfield along with my dad who sat me down and cared enough to put me on the path that straightened me out. Your father said two things to me that I will never forget. 1. Be kind to people on your way up, Towny, because you will see them on your way down. 2. Care for and love your players, it will go beyond the wins and losses. I took that advice as part of my change in philosophy and I am forever indebted to him. I am very happy that you feel he would be pleased by me being recognized for this award and I'm glad the family feels the same way. God bless y'all and give Jeremy my best. See you in January if not before if the good Lord is willing.

9/22/06 7:44 p.m.

Thanks again for all the thoughts, kind words, and inspiration that this web site has provided me and my family during this third battle with cancer. I have some good news from my last C.A.T. scan... tumors in both lungs are down by 33% and I can live with the side effects, although I'm a funny-looking bald guy. Ha-ha...I think we have it on the run. Thanks for all the PMs and emails and positive energy shown me during the last 5 years...you probably get tired of hearing about it, but I'm truly indebted to this baseball community... My family sends their best to all of you who have lifted us up during some rough times off the diamond. Thanks Blaster, MN-Mom for your support and Midlo-Dad it was a pleasure meeting you and your son in Richmond...he has a bright future and I look forward to following him. Thanks again everyone. Towny quote: I have survived to laugh at the odds and to live my life so well that death will tremble to take me.

8/11/06 10:23 a.m.

My family and I were absolutely overwhelmed by the event Thursday evening held at Greenbrier Christian Academy. I would also like to thank Bob Nichols, Ron Smith and Gary Lavelle, and many others for their efforts and friendship on my behalf. The photos given and stories told had me running the gamut of feelings and emotions from laughter to love. So many times over the last 5 years my teammates, friends, past players, parents and baseball community as a whole have rallied to my aid spiritually, financially, and emotionally. In spite of my circumstances presently I have got to be one of the luckiest guys around and have so much to be grateful for. I am rich in friends and relationships. I am grateful to so many and truly humbled by the words spoken the other night and if the purpose was to lift my spirits, consider the evening a complete success for my family and I know this that there is no quit in me and I expect a miracle. I have no plans on just rolling over. I picture myself coming back from this and seeing another spring of Baseball. Once again thanks so much to all who had a part in the most memorable evening of my life.

1/1/07 5:07 p.m.

I am sorry I have not been up to responding to the post from those who were present on the night of the O.D.U. banquet. My family and I have just been amazed at the response from all of you from that evening. I wish that I could have stayed and socialized to the late night with all of you. I hit a wall shortly after the speech and family felt that it was time to get me out of there. O.D.U. did an incredible job in its treatment of me and my family and it was a lifetime moment for the Townsends. I'm still expecting a miracle and believe God is involved with me in my healing. It's great to see spring is here and boys are off to the ball fields again and the boys of summer are gearin' up play…So many have asked regarding my speech about my closing remarks/statement, here it is...TALENT IS GOD GIVEN, BE THANKFUL. FAME IS MAN GIVEN, BE HUMBLE, CONCEIT IS SELF-GIVEN, BE VERY CAREFUL...God bless to all and thanks to so many!!!

–Towny

3/1/07 4:33 p.m.

R.I.P. Towny Townsend

Earlier today, Towny Townsend passed away. I just got the call a short while ago. REDBIRD5. 4/4/07 3:28 p.m.

Towny Townsend and his world changed in 2002 when he was diagnosed with cancer. The combination of chemotherapy and radiation pioneered close to 60 years before by Babe Ruth was thought to have cleared Towny of cancer. Still, just before the five-year mark of when patients can feel confident enough to be cancer-free, Towny learned it had returned and with more aggressiveness. The cancer spread from the throat area to the tongue, brain, and lungs. Towny had more fights and surgeries to go.

Townsend was not a smoker or drinker. "People used to ask Towny if he wanted a nipple for his beer; so no, he was not a drinker," said Cathy Townsend. The images of ballplayers, back in the day, with a wad of chew or dip, were not the picture of Towny either. "When Towny was first in the Minor Leagues, the other players made him stuff his mouth full of tobacco and hold it in until he threw up. That was the end of that," explained Cathy Townsend.

Towny was a tall, lean, and clean-living man. A younger and less mature version of Towny was passionate, hypercompetitive, and letting his fiery temper get the best of him, willing to fight at the drop of a hat. It was said Towny would occasionally acknowledge his behaviors as "the only person to be thrown out of a baseball game as a player, as a coach, as a parent, and as a spectator."

As Towny grew older, he strengthened his relationship with God and perhaps even began to mellow to a certain degree.

We may never really know if Towny was scared at the prospect of not recovering. Yet, even as part of his tongue and a piece of his leg were removed, Towny carried on.

"The doctors thought he had beaten it, and then it came back. Towny was surprised it came back the second time," explained Cathy Townsend. Towny went through with the surgery and then more chemo. He was still in chemo when he passed away. By the time he died, the cancer had spread everywhere, throat, brain, and lungs. His speech was majorly affected, and he started his speeches by saying, "Okay, I sound like Donald Duck, but I have important stuff to tell you." "Towny tried to have a good sense of humor about it," explained Cathy Townsend.

Speech affected, that was fine. Body compromised through chemotherapy and radiation, no problem as he would throw batting practice after batting practice to the players. In his mind, he would not show or burden others with his own pain and fears. His battle and pain were his own, and he refused to let others think otherwise of him as a competitive, demanding, and caring coach…for them.

Towny fought cancer hard, convinced he was going to beat it. But, Towny said in his Bud Metheny Award acceptance speech not long before he died, "Cancer picked the wrong guy to try to beat." Nevertheless, the "never give up" attitude was there to the end, and he rarely would share his fears or concerns or let his guard down to friends and family. The end was near, and perhaps even Towny knew it.

After he retired from a long baseball career, Gary Lavelle became one of Towny Townsend's best friends. Gary Lavelle is a strongly religious person. Over the years, before and after Towny was diagnosed with cancer, he discussed religion and helped Towny with his spiritual journey.

"Towny and I had good talks. He loved the Lord and became very close to Jesus by the end of his life. I think his faith was great comfort in the end to him," Gary Lavelle said. "I loved Towny. He was a great guy and a coach," added Gary Lavelle.

Greenbrier Christian Academy baseball has had 12 Baseball State Championships since Gary Lavelle first took the program in 1989. Eleven of the 12 are under Gary Lavelle, and the 12th is under Towny Townsend.

Gary Lavelle as a former All-Star pitcher, retired to Hampton Roads. He took a couple years off and figured he would take a small baseball program and try to make it a winner and then, in time, step away for other opportunities. Gary Lavelle did just that, with Towny Townsend eventually taking over as head coach at Greenbrier Christian. Gary Lavelle became a pitching coach in the New York Yankees Organization for five years and came back. To some, it may have looked like Towny Townsend was fired, quit, or squeezed out by Gary Lavelle.

Cathy Townsend knows Towny Townsend did not quit, and he wanted to keep coaching at Greenbrier, but he was not able to. Gary Lavelle, even years later, doesn't like the perception that he pushed Towny Townsend out of a job.

"When I came back from coaching with the Yankees, I was not coming back to coach baseball at Greenbriar. I did not want to be the coach. It was Towny's job," said Gary Lavelle. "Then I got a call from Greenbrier saying Towny was not going to be the head coach. Towny was one of my best friends. There was no way I wanted to interfere with what he was doing," explained Gary Lavelle.

But Towny Townsend was deep into a fight for his life that he was determined to win. His nature on the baseball field was tough and tenacious, but cancer is one Mean Son of Bitc*. Loyalty and friendships ran deep with Towny, and his friends felt the same.

"Towny fought that thing as hard as anyone I've ever seen in my 62 years, and I saw him break at the end," said Matt Sinnen. "We were still in the end, and he hugged me and told me 'to take care of his kids.' I loved Towny Townsend. I owe him quite a bit, if not everything, outside of my family to the game of baseball and Towny Townsend," explained Matt Sinnen.

"I went to that house the night before he passed away and talked with him. He said to me, if you could ever do anything for my family, I would appreciate it because they're going to really need some help," said Gary Wright. "Matt (Sinnen) and I really kind of tried to look out after the Townsends," explained Gary Wright.

Towny must have known his time was running short, or the cancer would claim his body one day soon. The night before Towny passed away, he was inducted into the Norfolk Sports Hall of Fame. Towny was not feeling well and had his wife, Cathy accepted the award on his behalf. Towny spent part of his last night alive firing up the internet and checking out how his players were doing in college and professional baseball. Towny had his sister over to be with him, and Gary Wright stopped by to talk. Towny called his oldest son, Sean, that night and spoke. "I wanted to outlive my mother, and I did that. I am not worried about you and your brother. I know you guys are going to be okay."

"He passed away the next day," said Sean Townsend.

Towny Townsend wanted to be at the Norfolk Sports Club to accept the Norfolk Sports Hall of Fame Award, to see friends made throughout his long baseball journey, but Towny felt death closing in and was preparing to ask his wife a question he never once asked her during his long battle with cancer. But he finally did the morning he died.

"I know if there was any way he could have gone that night, he would have done it. Later that night, I sat with him, and we talked while I held the trophy, but he was really tired. The next morning, he just asked me, 'So do you think I'm going to die?' I think he must have known. I told him I don't know when anybody's time is, I don't know when it is yours, and then I kissed him and left to work. I think he felt it. I came back, and he was gone," said Cathy Townsend.

Chase Townsend is very much like his father, and he felt lost without his father. However, Sean is a more talkative person and more willing to share feelings and emotions.

Sean Townsend had someone to help him grieve. "Sean was the Junior Varsity Coach for Coach Lee. Coach Lee lost his father about the same age as Sean was, and knew what he was going through. He was a Godsend for Sean, but Chase was the one that was lost. He holds everything inside," said Cathy Townsend.

Everyone deals with stress and grief in their own way, no way is more valid than another, but sometimes emotions can create scary incidents. Chase was one to hold his feelings in, and when he was 21 years old, watching a Major League game bought on memories of his father and a possible panic attack.

"Chase went with some friends to go see a Washington Nationals game and thought he had a heart attack. They rushed him to the hospital," said Cathy Townsend. "I think it was sitting at the game and thinking about his father," explained Cathy Townsend.

Losing Towny was hard on the family. But just talking about him or hearing others talk about him softens the pain.

"It helps to talk, it's hard, but it does help to hear people talk about him," said Cathy Townsend.

As Towny, Cathy, Sean, and Chase grappled with the fear and uncertainty of the cancer fight for years, the struggle and strength shown are still remembered and admired by B.J. Upton.

"Coach 'T' was a great man, a great man to know, a great man to talk with, he was a father, a coach, a brother, he was whatever the communities needed him to be," said B.J. Upton.

Even as B.J. Upton was going through the whirlwind of being a baseball prodigy and compared as a faster Derek Jeter with more power, or the next Willie Mays, B.J. Upton saw and felt everything around him involving Towny and his family as he played for Towny in high school.

"You talk about tough; I mean I may have had it tough, but Sean and Chase, they really had it tougher on them than anybody, and Miss Cathy, just always quiet, nice as can be, never said much about it and always had a smile on her face. If you didn't know about Coach T's cancer, you would never know about it from them. They are the strongest people I've ever met in my life," said B.J. Upton.

When Towny first was diagnosed with cancer, it hit David Wright hard.

"It was the first time I knew somebody going through something like that. I was as a kid. It was hard personally, a pretty difficult time. But you would never know he was sick, except for toward the end, by looking at him or talking to him. He never wanted to talk about himself, his sickness, or be asked questions like 'how do you feel' or 'how were you doing' or about the treatments he was going through. He always wanted to talk about baseball or talk about you. If you asked about himself, he would change it back to you or something baseball-related, changing the subject because he never wanted you to feel sorry for him or treat him differently because of how he sounded or how he looked at the time. It was never when he was sick about him. It was always, you know, 'how's your swing' or 'what are you thinking about this?' It was good because you're not built for seeing somebody else who did so much for you go through something like that as a young kid. It was always good to have baseball in common. I didn't know how to be compassionate for an adult going through something like that, but he taught me in a way and made it easier and more comfortable with his selflessness," explained David Wright.

Even as the loss is felt by David Wright and others, the feeling of a continued legacy holds strong.

"We lost a tremendous baseball person, but I think it's almost like you look at like Bill Parcells or how you would look at a Bill Belichick and all the branches. Towny had so many people under him and learning from him. I think we're still seeing the effects of Towny Townsend. Even to this day, you still have disciples of Towny. His reach was far and wide. Towny cast a wide net, and so many people learned from him and are still teaching, including his son, and a lot of his son's friends got into coaching," said David Wright.

Years removed from looking up to Michael Cuddyer in high school, David Wright still sees Michael Cuddyer as a person doing the right things and as a person to admire and following the coaching philosophies of Coach Townsend.

"Michael Cuddyer is into coaching; he has a kid going into high school. I think Towny's work and influence will live on at least four lifetimes. Michael will teach his kid the same things that Towny taught him, and Michael's kids can teach their kids the same thing Towny taught his father. Hopefully, it's never-ending, because I didn't fully appreciate it until looking back on it now about what you can teach players," explained David Wright.

The lessons David Wright talks about as the legacy of the Splendid 6 are a small part about baseball. The legacy is the pride of doing something seemingly impossible, and doing it the right way.

"Not to brag, but you know these guys always carry themselves the right way. You can look at them, the Mark Reynolds, the Ryan Zimmermans and it remains. The Michael Cuddyers, it was always about giving back to the community; it was always playing the game the right way, it was playing the game hard, it was never making the news for doing the wrong things. I think a lot of that was through those life lessons learned on those fields, and hopefully, we'll continue to teach our kids and our grandkids those lessons down the road," said David Wright.

The Blasters are on the way back. Former Blasters players remaining in the area plan to bring back Towny Townsend's brainchild and further the Blasters legacy.

"My son is only one year old now, but if he ever gets into baseball, if he wants to play, the perfect team name would be the Blasters. We could even have the East Coast Blasters and the West Coast Blasters face off. I still have the jerseys and the t-shirts," explained David Wright.

David Wright is a long time removed from youth baseball and climbed to the highest points of the Major League Baseball, but the Blasters, coaches, and those youth teammates still bring back strong memories.

"That's how much that team and that coaching staff meant to me. I didn't make it to where I'm at without them. If Towny and the other coaches were in front of me today, I would say 'thank you' for what they did, not only in baseball but for me as a person and for a lot of friends I had that were in the game," said David Wright.

David Wright did not understand the special, unique nature of the situations and environment he was blessed to be in as a youngster. But a long baseball career and seeing the paths of many other players around him that made it to the Major Leagues, he understands the edge and advantages he had from his baseball internship with his coaches.

"You get spoiled when you get a chance to be around those two men growing up on a pretty consistent basis. Like any other kid,

I think I took it for granted. Until Towny's not around or you're not around that culture as much as you used to be. I began to understand the amount of time, effort, money, and passion they put into the Blasters," said David Wright. "I know there was a lot of pride seeing their kids go on and play high school, college, and professional baseball. It was by luck I had the chance to meet Coach Townsend and Coach Erbe. It is no coincidence the Hampton Roads area became a baseball hotbed, and it would not have been a baseball hotbed without them," explained David Wright.

Not even Towny Townsend could predict the Splendid 6 in baseball. "I think even Towny himself was surprised at the results some of the players had," said Sean Townsend.

Towny Townsend, Allan Erbe, Manny Upton, Matt Sinnen, and Gary Wright, and other coaches cannot take all the credit for the Splendid 6 Tidewater Baseball Boys. Still, they certainly would be just as proud of what Towny Townsend wanted, and what all the coaches did to help make it happen. A person then a player. Coach Towny Townsend's legacy is the players and coaches he helped shape, and hopefully, it can continue down the line.

Even with Towny passing away, the respect held for him was evident and overwhelming. In life, Towny Townsend made people look at him and listen to him.

"I think Towny had a prolific presence like an aura almost around him when he walked on a Baseball diamond," said Matt Sinnen.

Even at his own funeral, the words of wisdom from Towny Townsend came through as those who loved and respected him gave channel to his voice once more.

To Rev. Randy Childress, the way Townsend modeled love, discipline, and perseverance, especially during his long struggle, will endure as his most lasting lessons. "Don't make people just admire you," Childress said. "Make them glad you were here."

The same words Towny Townsend ended his Hampton Roads Sports Hall of Fame induction were spoken out loud again to memorialize him. Townsend's favorite saying borrowed from the words of another great coach, NCAA Basketball Coach John Wooden.

"Talent is God-given; be thankful. Fame is man-given; be humble. Conceit is self-given; be very careful."

The funeral of Towny Townsend was overwhelming for Cathy Townsend.

"It's a blur to me. I remember being in the family room and coming out to the church and being overwhelmed by the number of people, and then I found out after the funeral that there was a whole other fellowship hall-full and they were watching it on closed-circuit television. It was over 600 people there. A full Sanctuary for the funeral, also the overflow room, it was totally insane," said Cathy Townsend.

Cathy Townsend's father passed away from prostate cancer just two weeks after Towny. Two of the most influential men of her life struck down so close in time by cancer. The losses were crushing, but she relied on some of her friends to get her through those times and is lucky enough to have them still and the family she expected to share with Towny as they grew old together.

"I have a close-knit group of girls I sang with growing up, with whom I still hang out. The girl I lived across the street from when I was five or six years old is still my best friend. I work, have my kids and grandkids; I'm happy," explained Cathy Townsend.

Over the years, fewer people have stopped Cathy Townsend on the street or while running errands. Phone calls and emails about Towny are less frequent. Instead, people move on and carry through with their own lives. Cathy Townsend is doing the same, with memories of Towny all around her in the house they once shared and where they raised their two boys.

A portrait she painted of Towny adorns their bedroom hallway. Despite the house being extensively remodeled, the side windows of the house's front door are still decorated with the stained-glass baseball theme from when Towny lived there. Their granddaughters want one of the stained-glass baseball players updated with a girl's ponytail. I think Towny, Pop-Pop "T" would approve. The Townsend home is still a place to find Towny.